Real World

Colouring Book

For Advanced Users & Adults

50 Images

Created From Real Life Photos
For You To Colour As You Please.

ISBN 978-0-359-86327-3

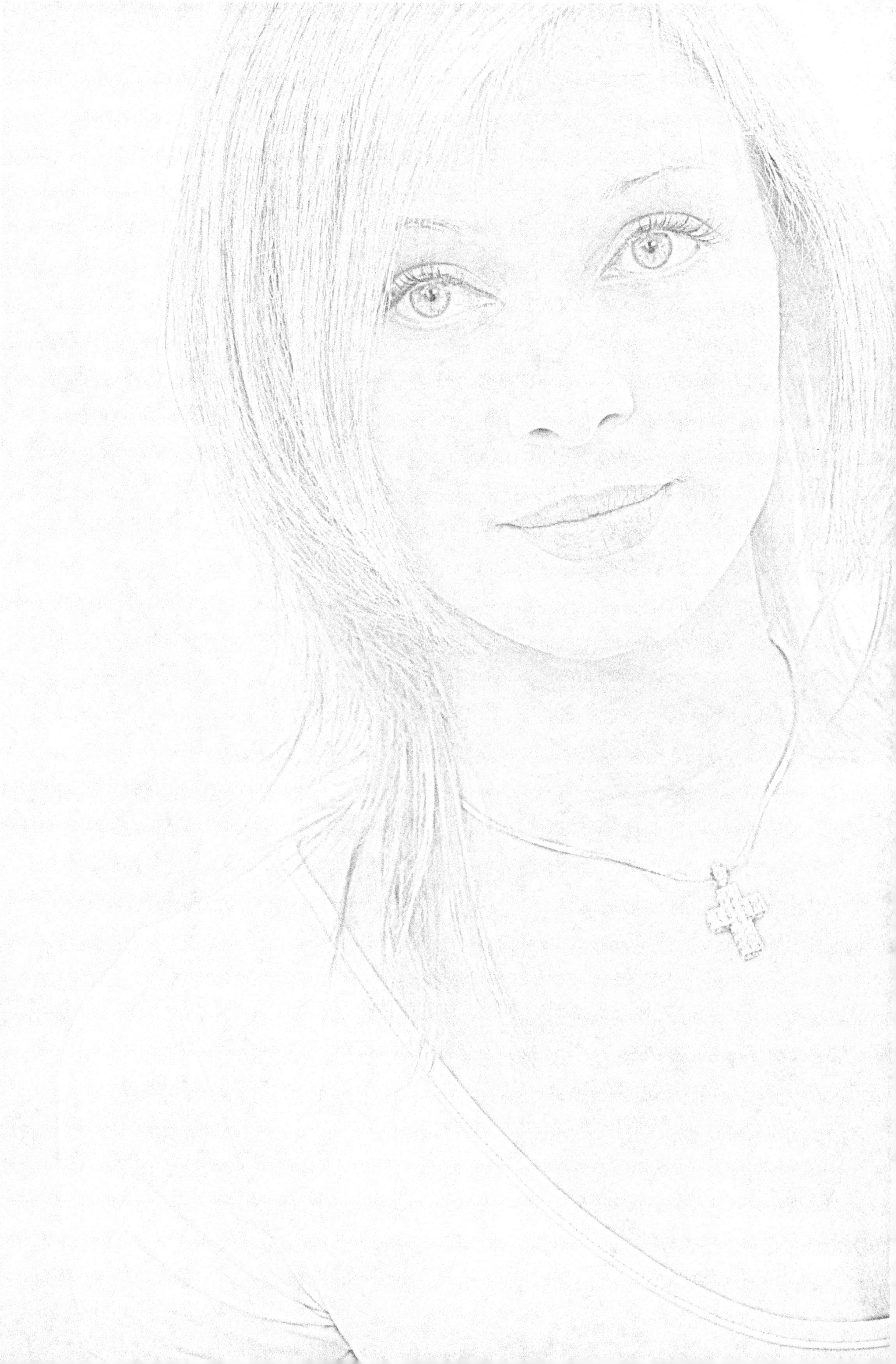

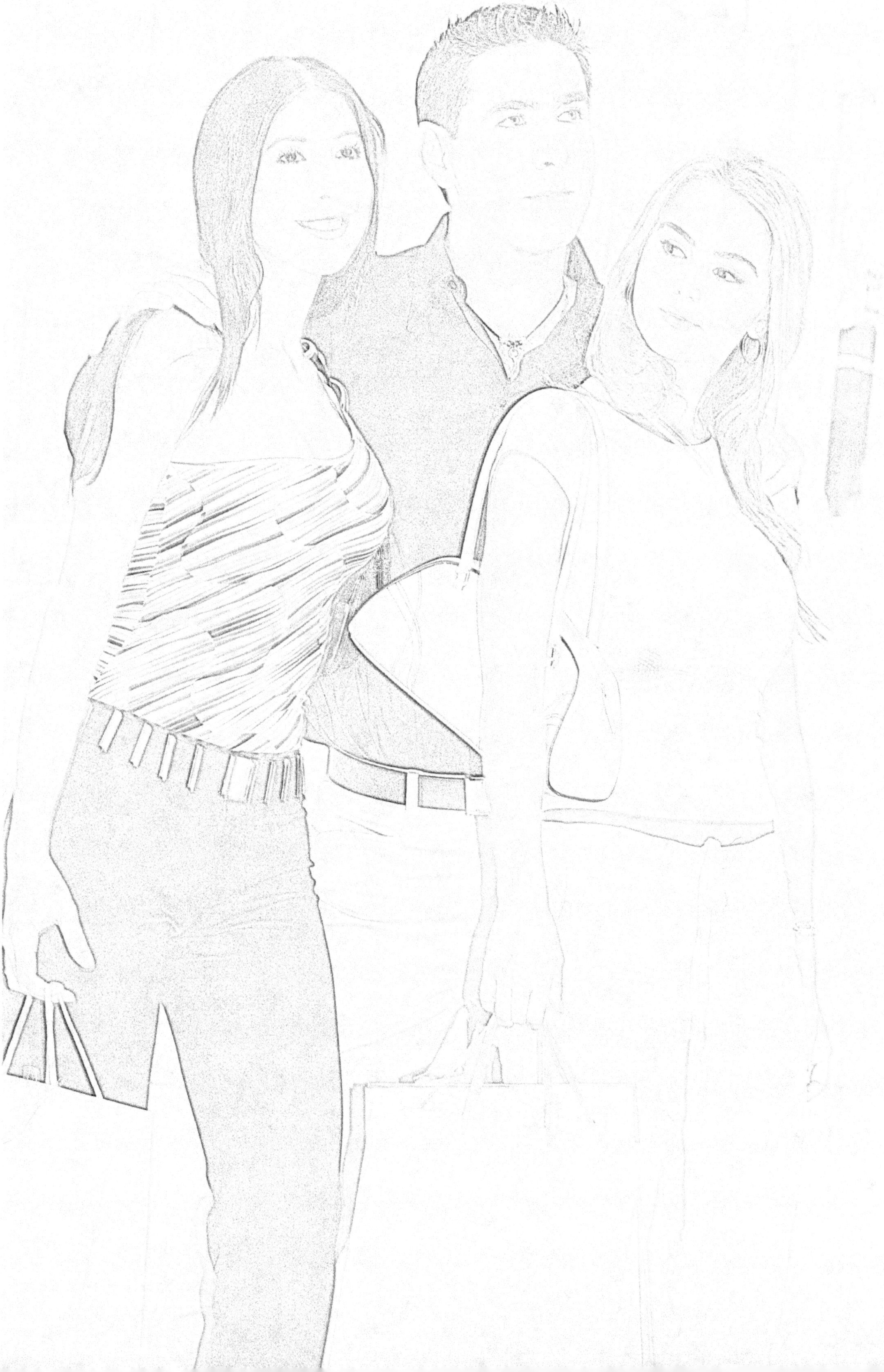

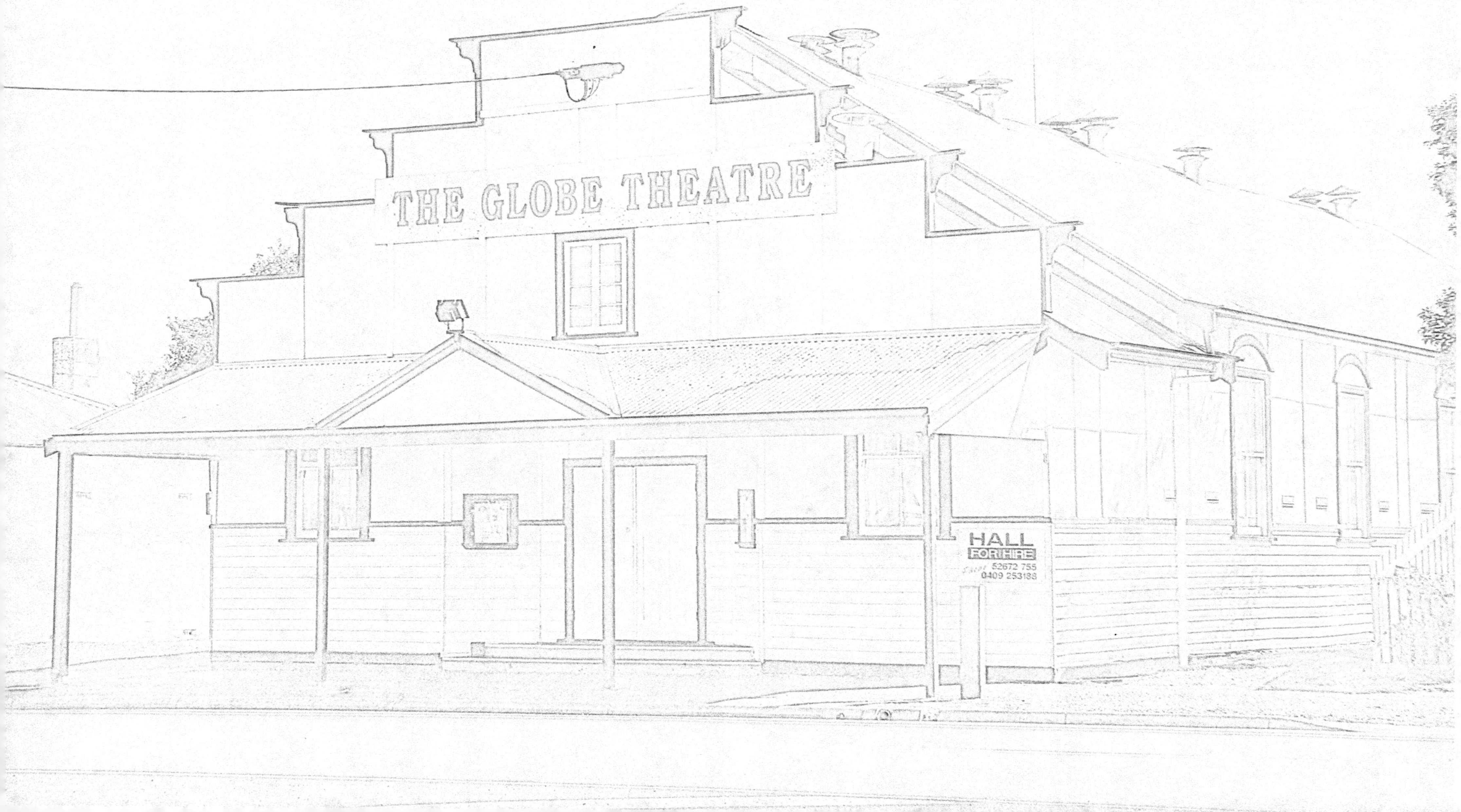
THE GLOBE THEATRE
HALL
FOR HIRE
52672 755
0409 253188

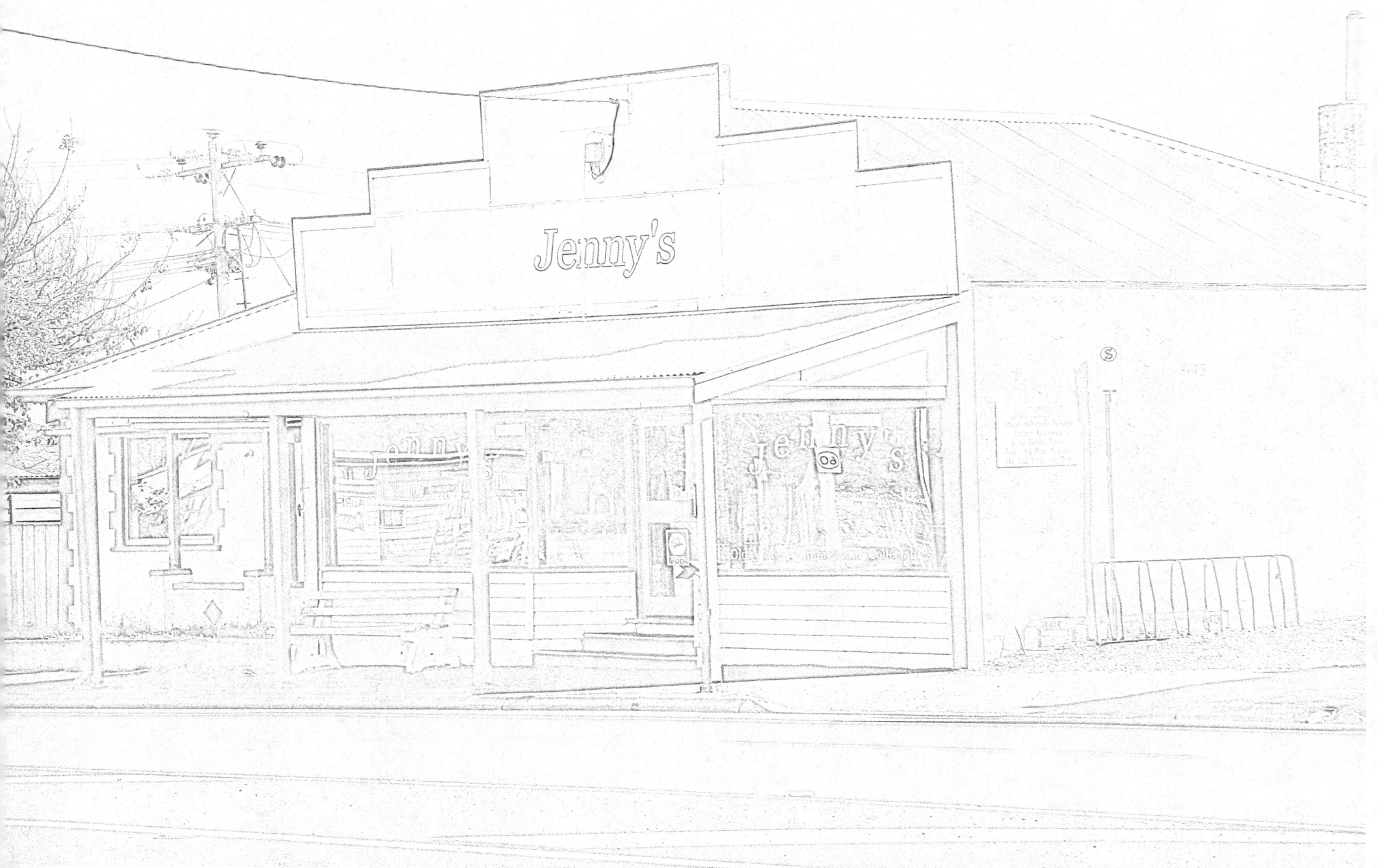
Jenny's

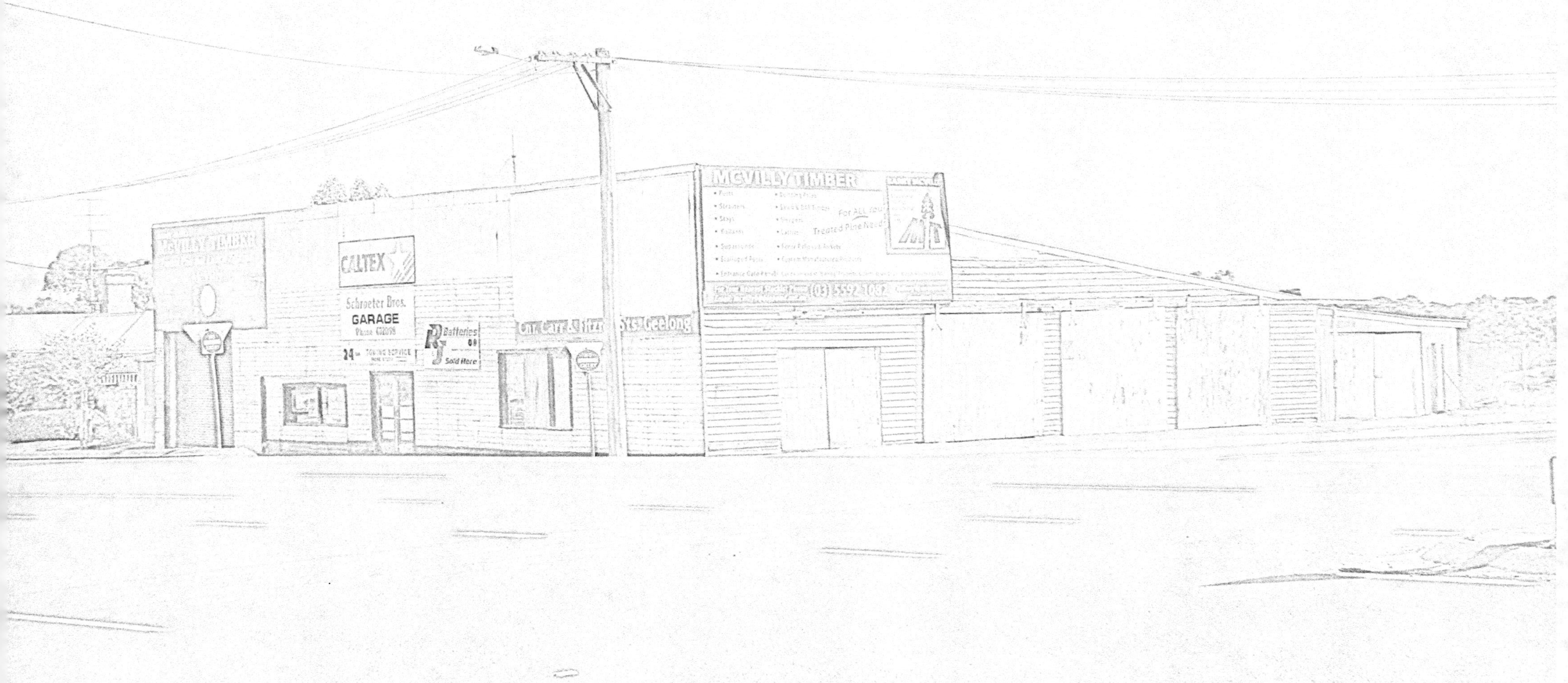
MCVILLY TIMBER
For ALL Your Treated Pine Needs
(03) 5592 1082
CALTEX
Schroeter Bros.
GARAGE
24
Batteries
Sold Here
Sts. Geelong

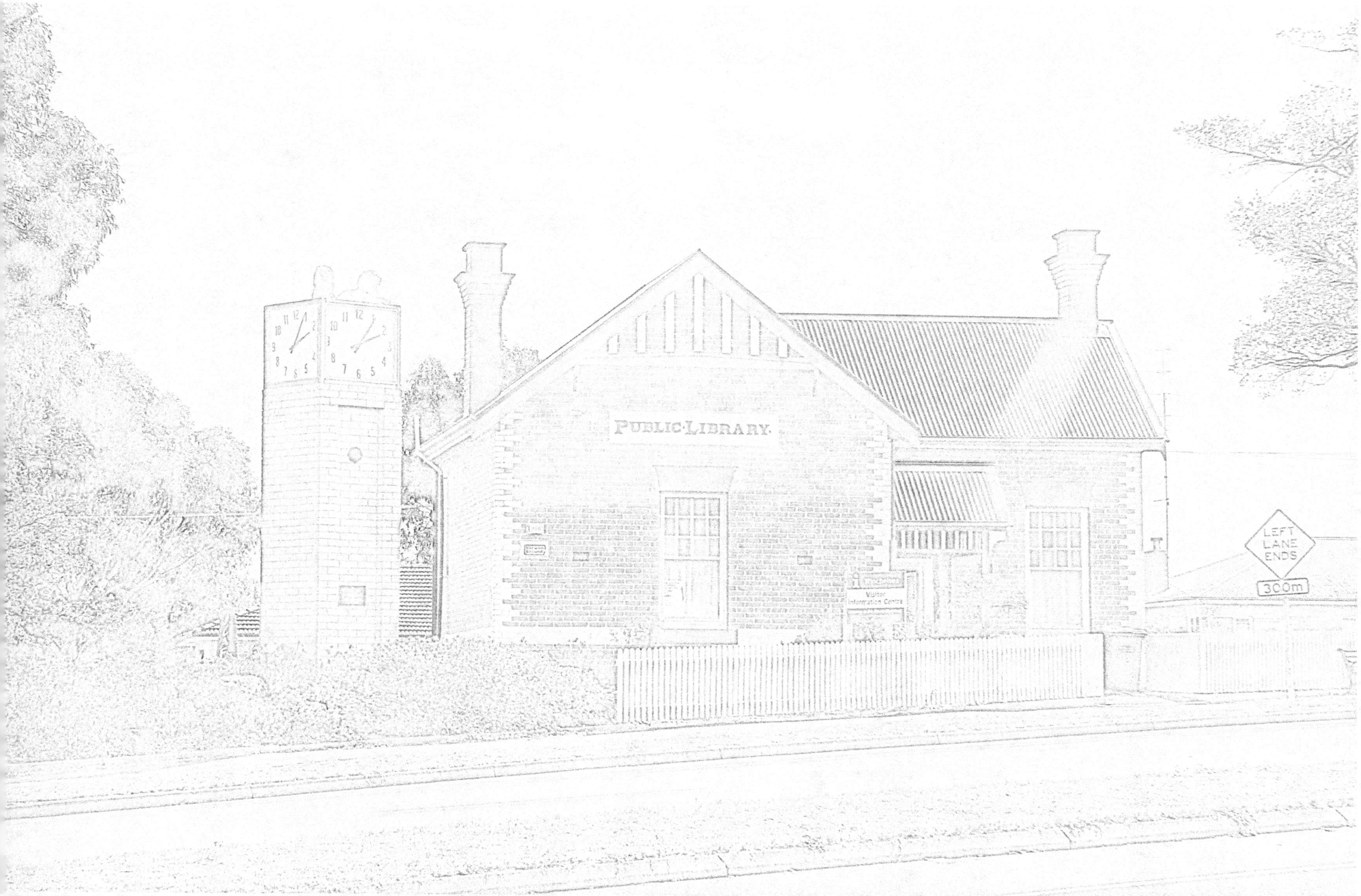
PUBLIC·LIBRARY.
Visitor Information Centre
LEFT LANE ENDS
300m

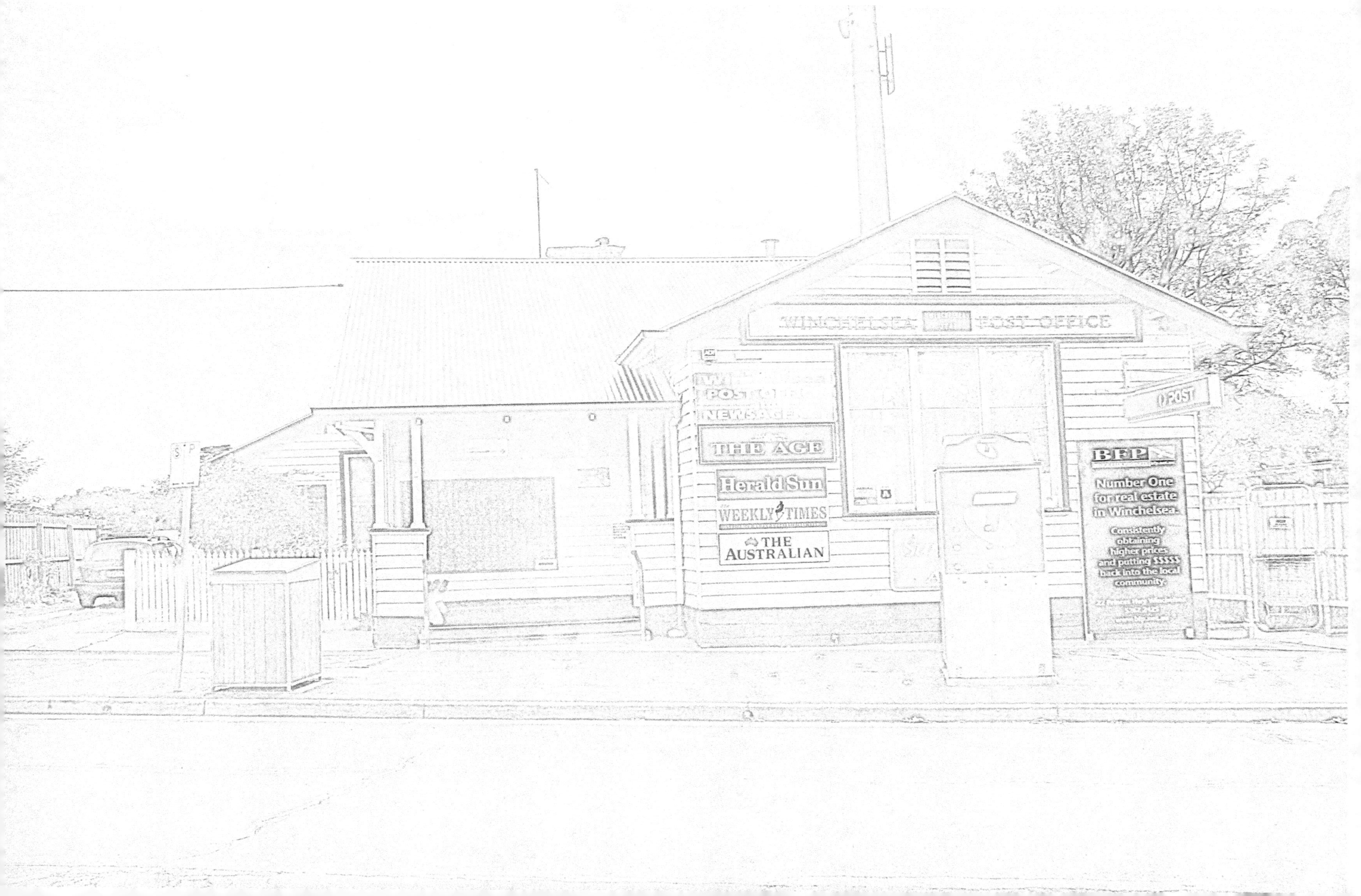
WINCHELSEA POST OFFICE
NEWSAGENT
THE AGE
Herald Sun
WEEKLY TIMES
THE AUSTRALIAN
POST
BFP
Number One for real estate in Winchelsea.
Consistently obtaining higher prices and putting $$$$$ back into the local community.

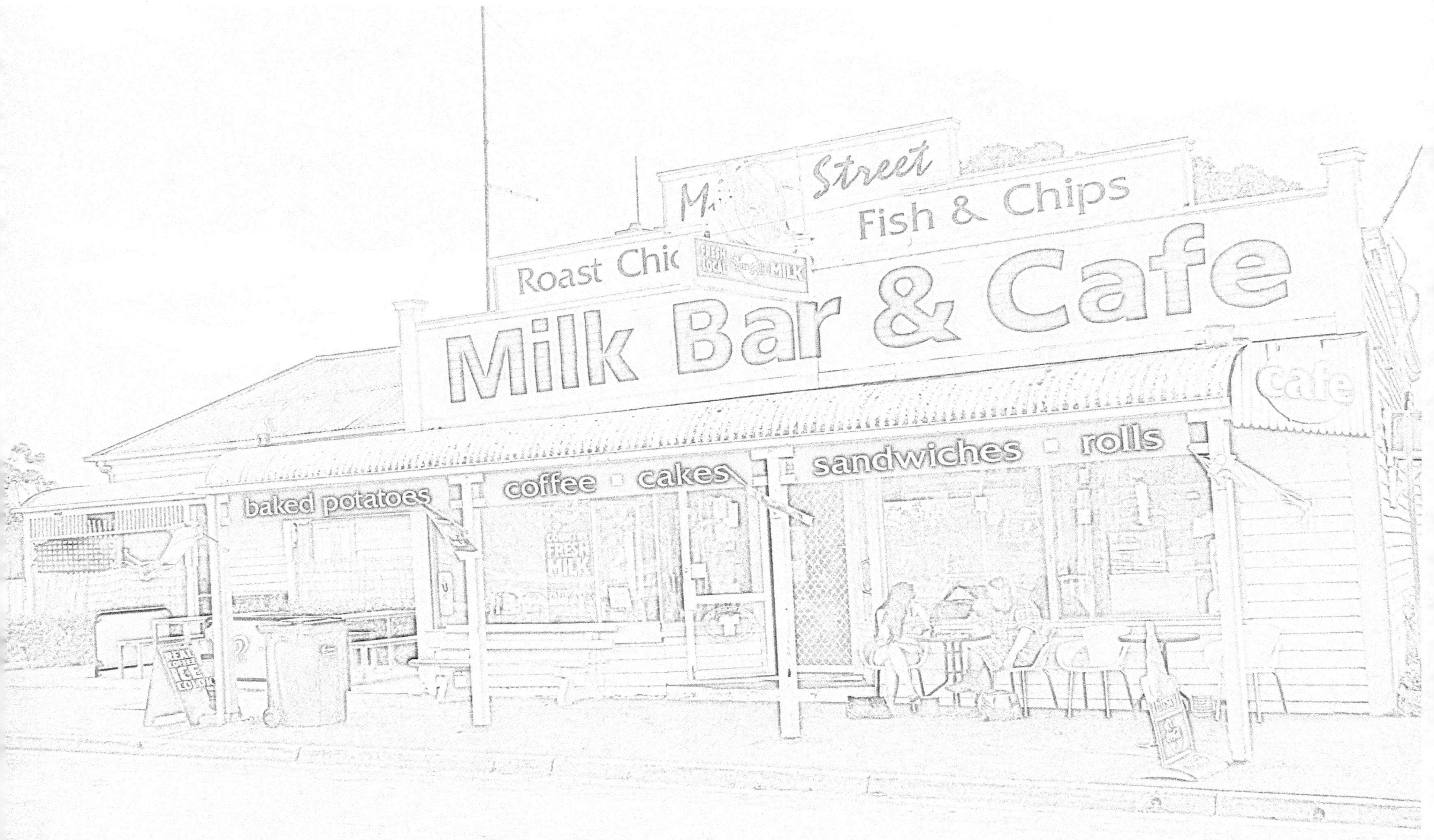
Street
Fish & Chips
Roast Chic
FRESH LOCAL MILK
Milk Bar & Cafe
cafe
baked potatoes
coffee
cakes
sandwiches
rolls
FRESH MILK
REAL COFFEE ICE COLD

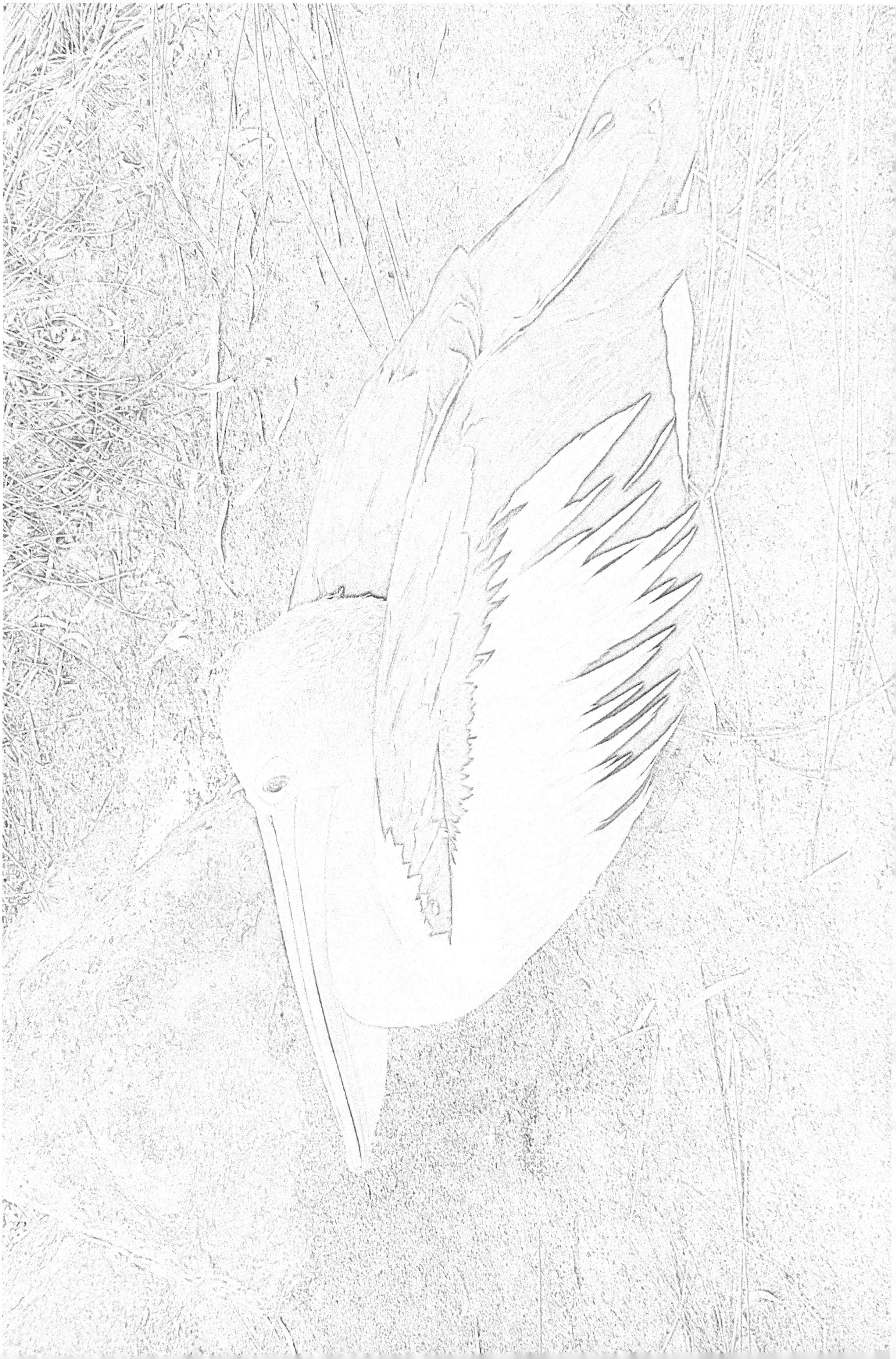

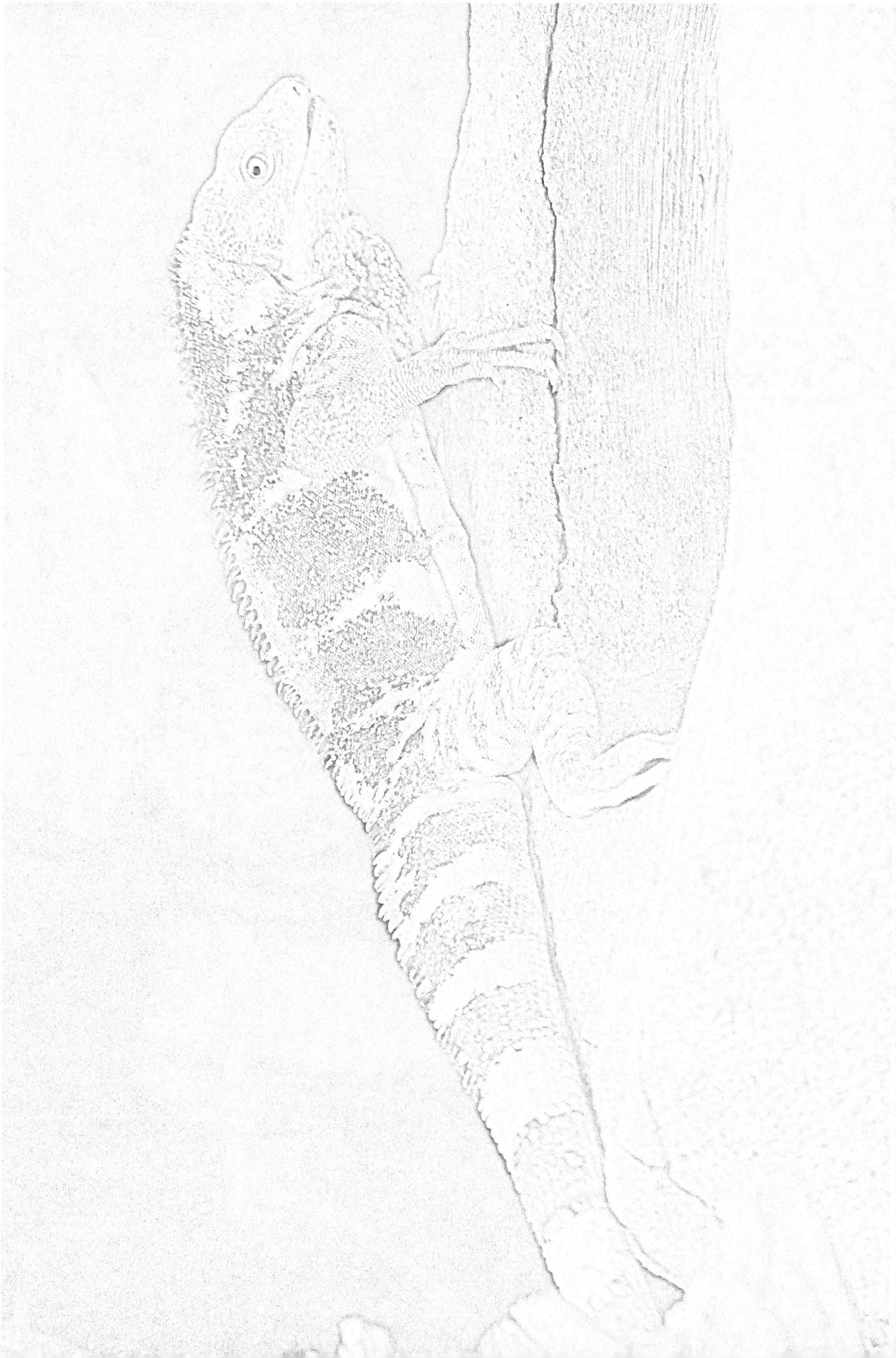

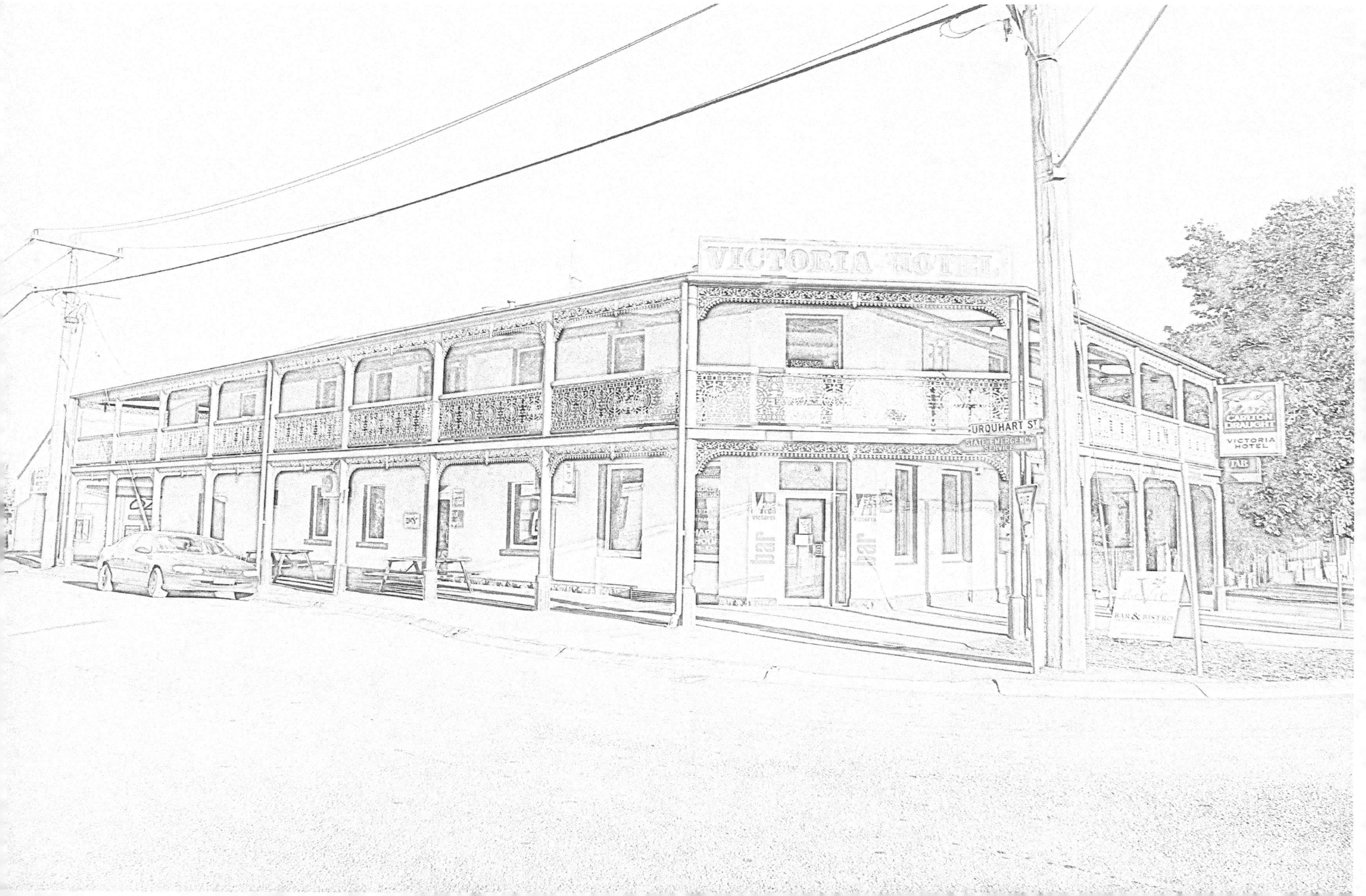
VICTORIA HOTEL
URQUHART ST
STATE EMERGENCY SERVICE
CARLTON DRAUGHT
VICTORIA HOTEL
TAB
BAR & BISTRO

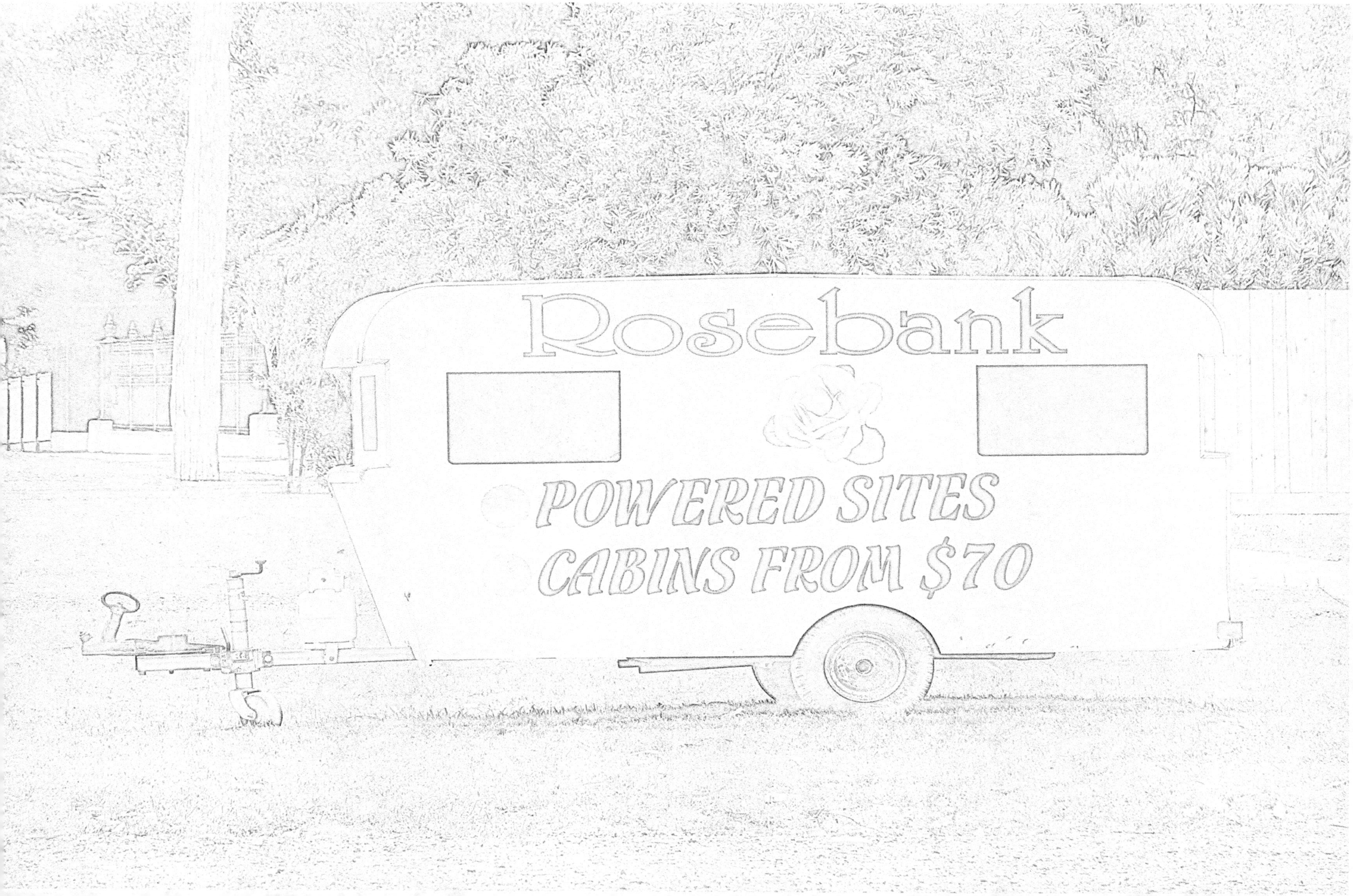
Rosebank
POWERED SITES
CABINS FROM $70

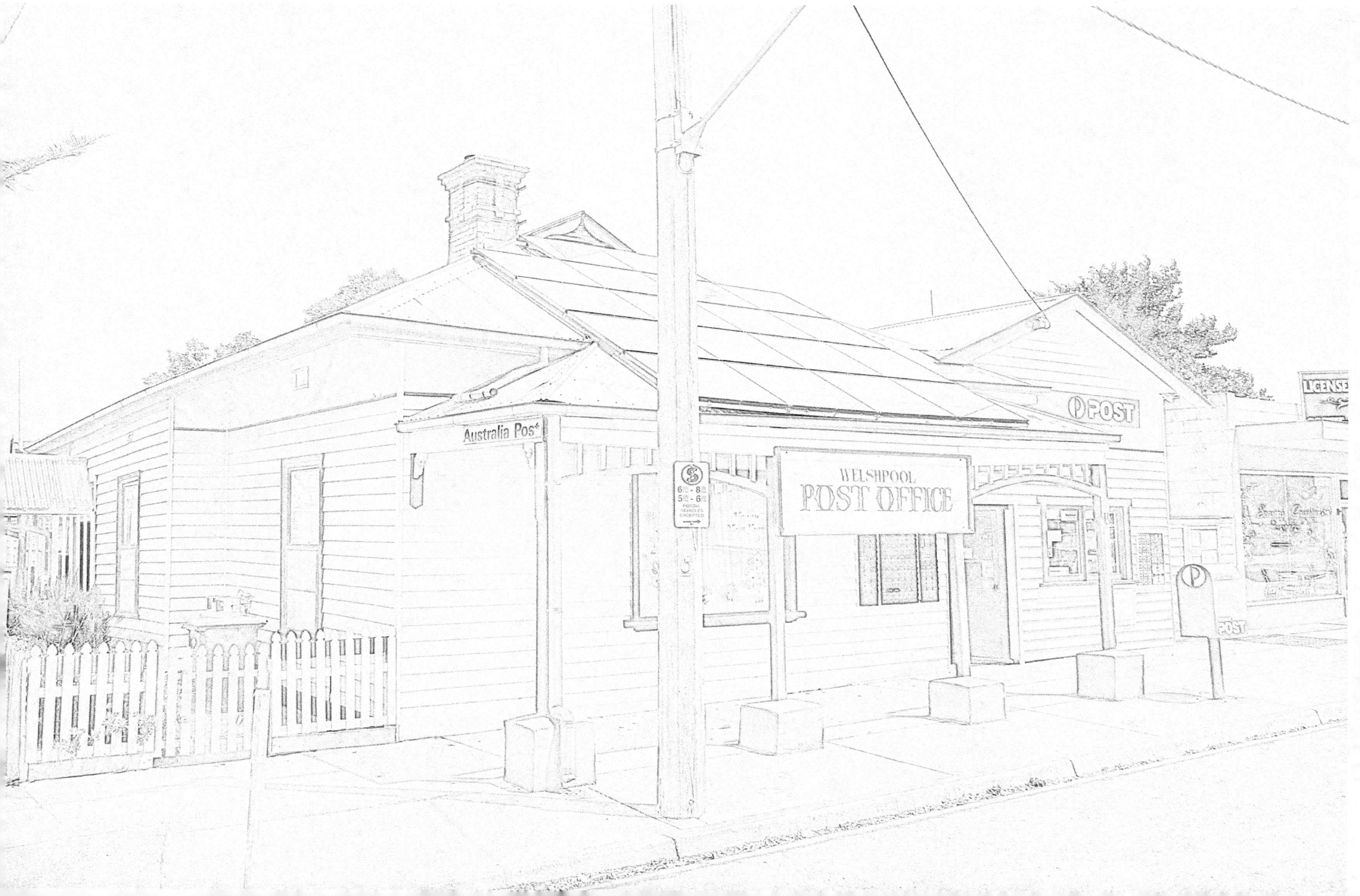
Australia Pos
WELSHPOOL
POST OFFICE
POST
POST

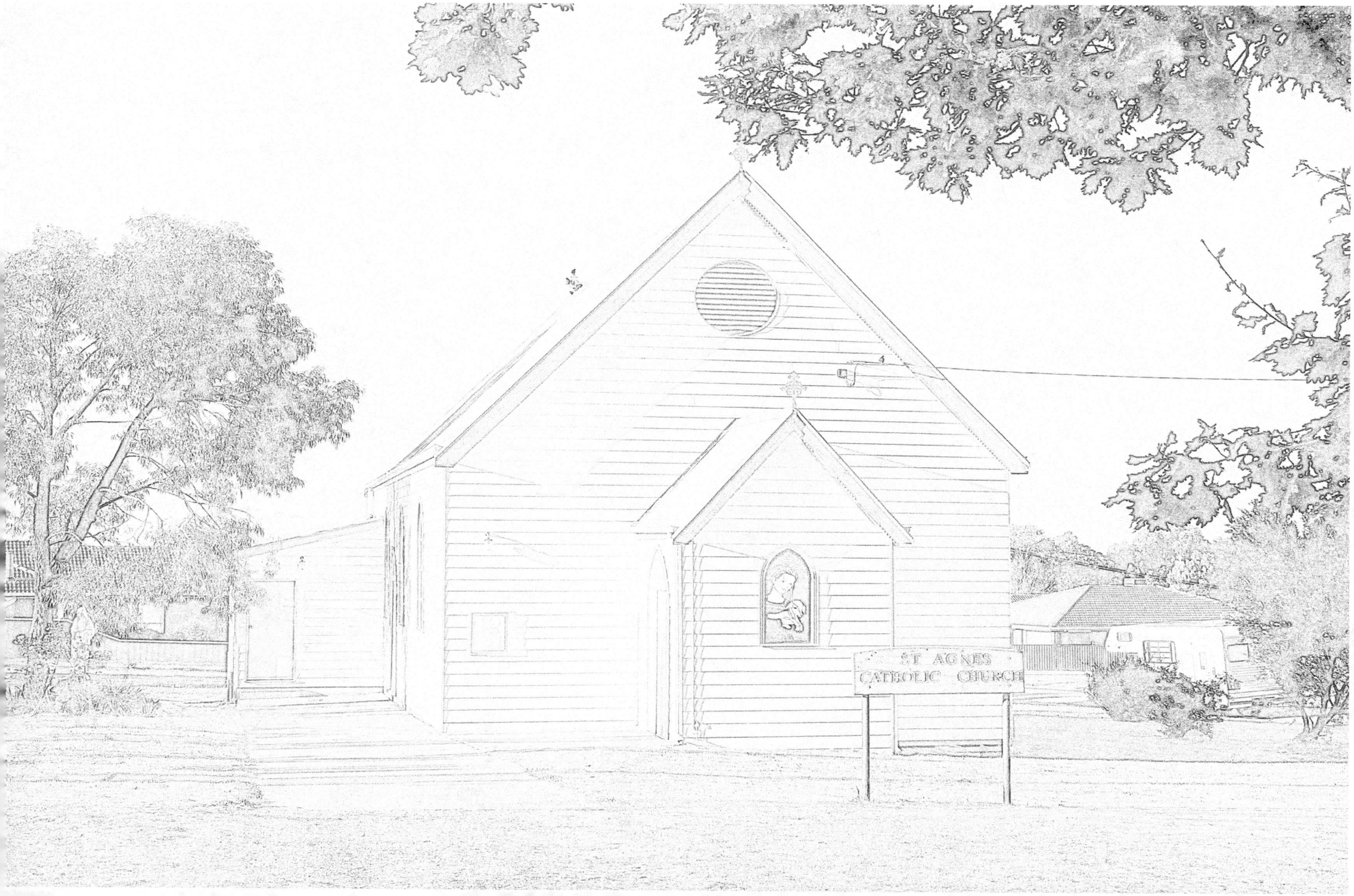
ST AGNES
CATHOLIC CHURCH

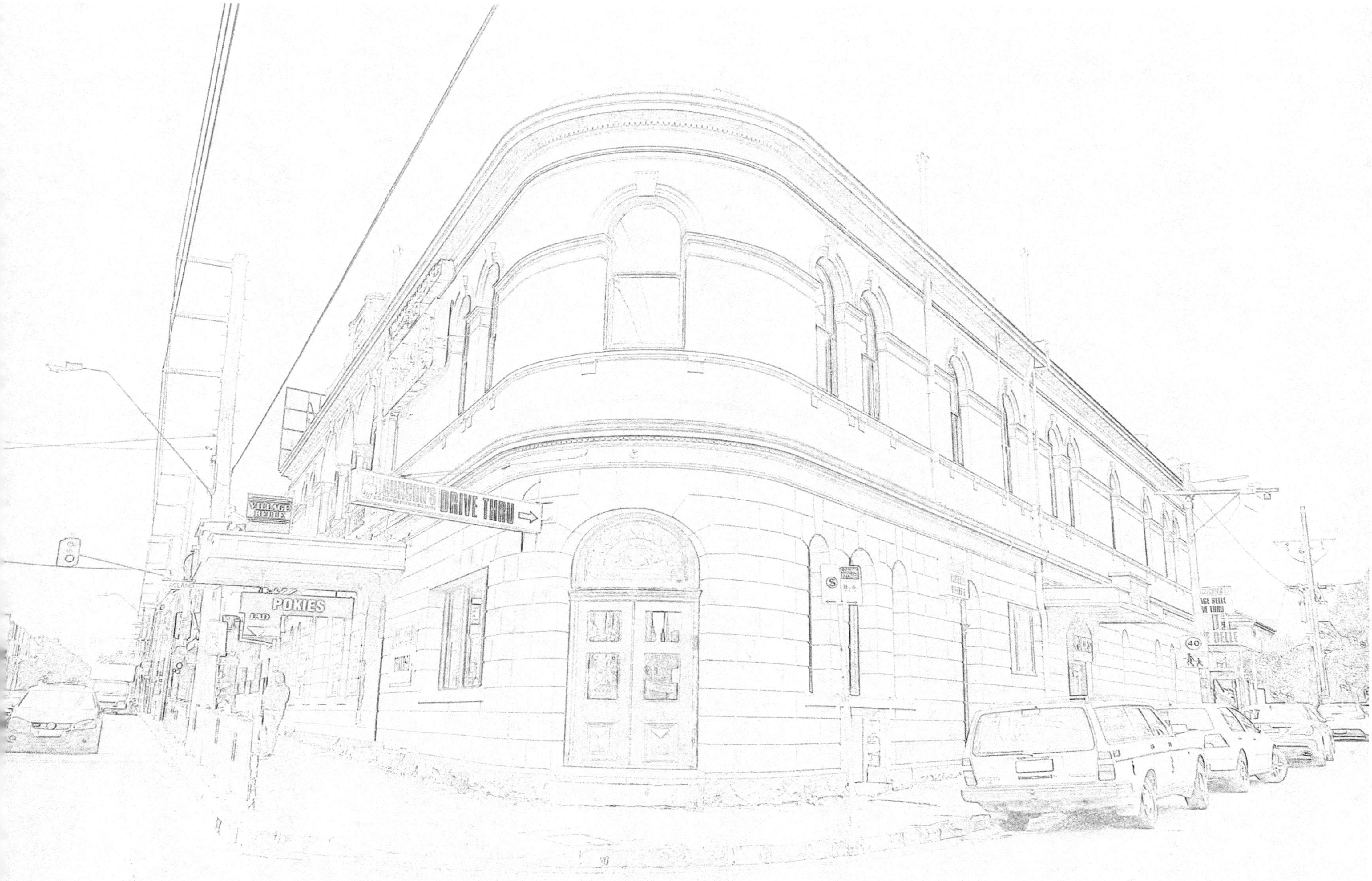

DRIVE THRU
POKIES
40

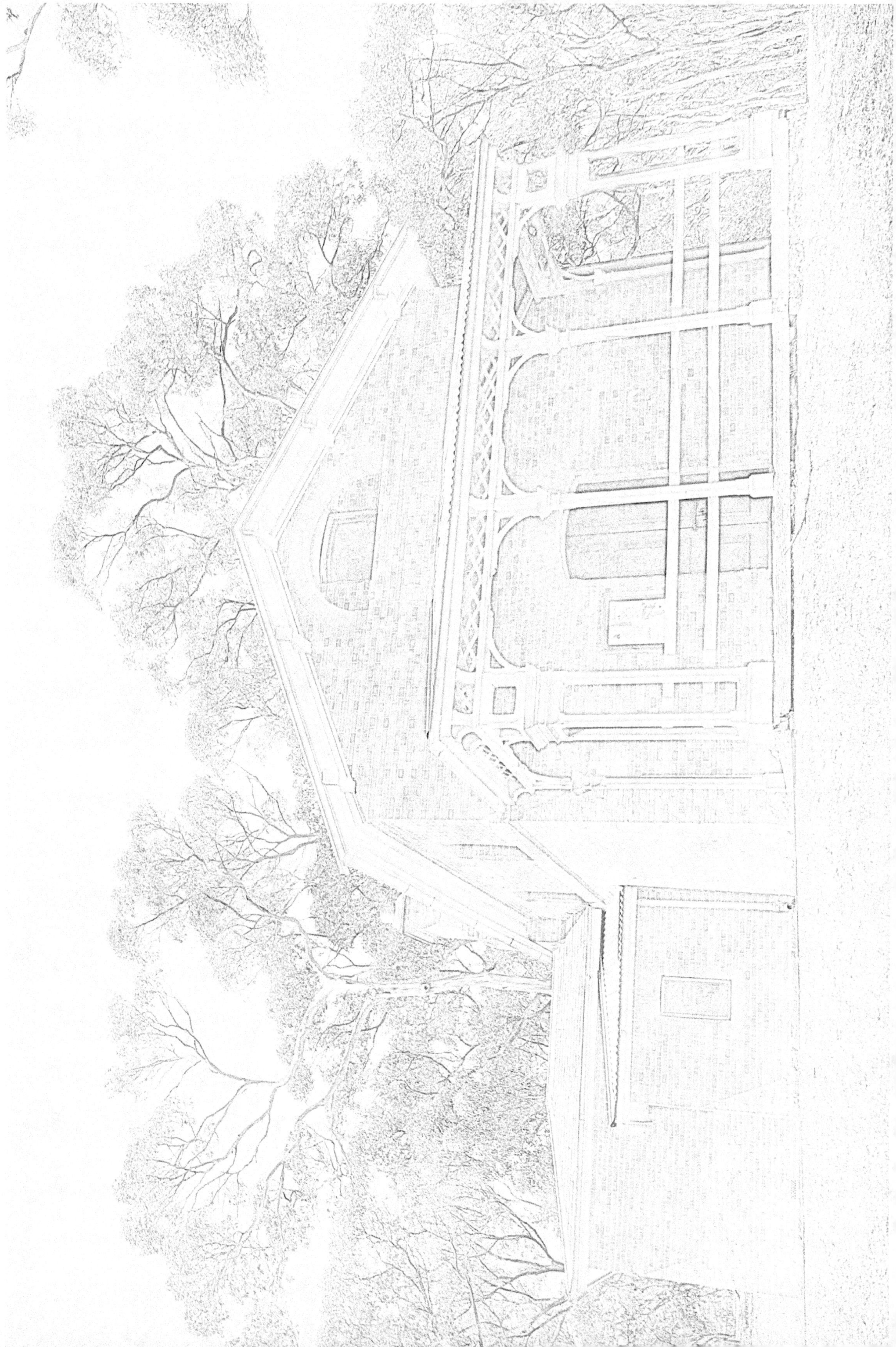

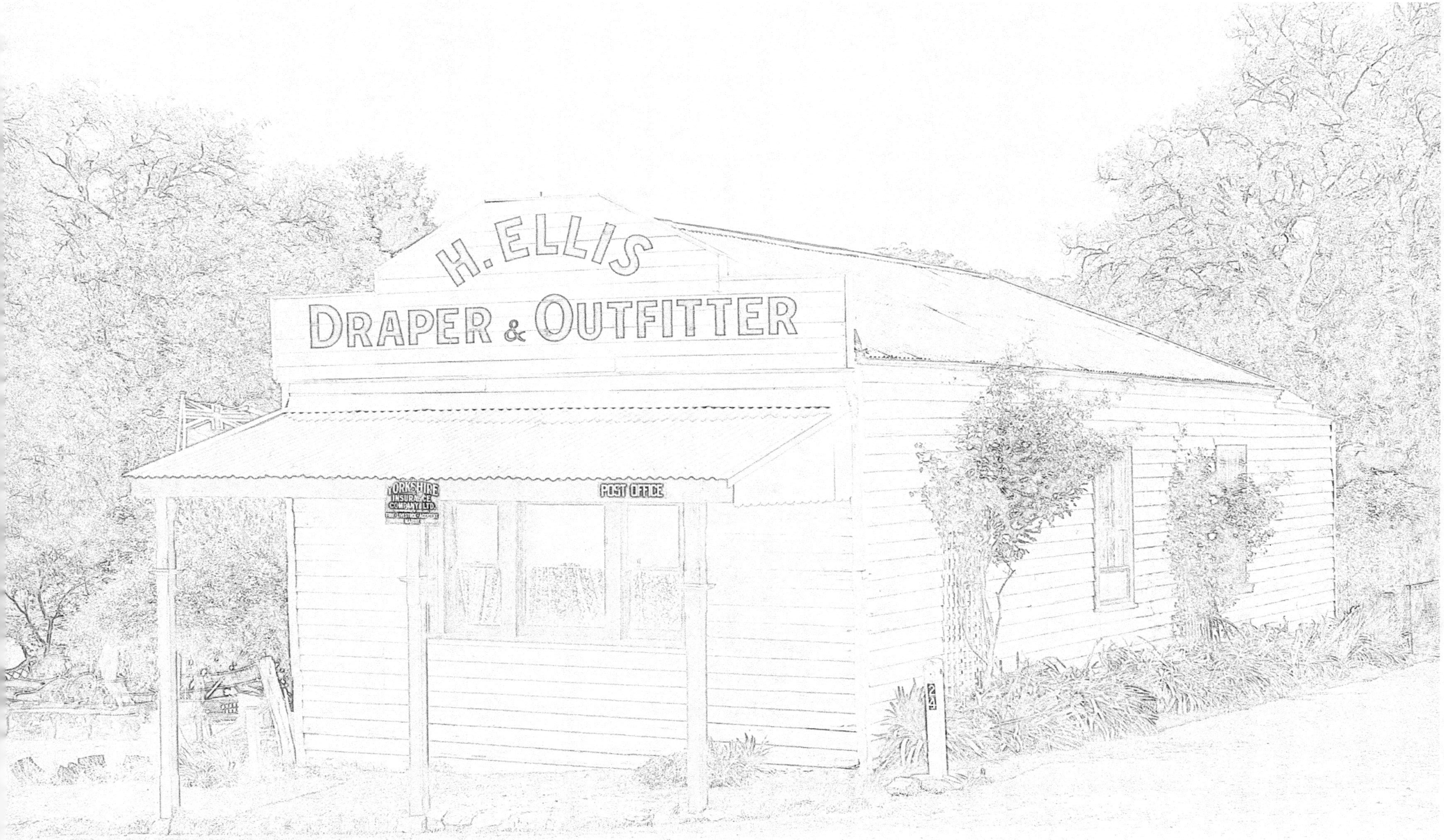
H. ELLIS
DRAPER & OUTFITTER
POST OFFICE
YORKSHIRE
INSURANCE
COMPANY LTD.

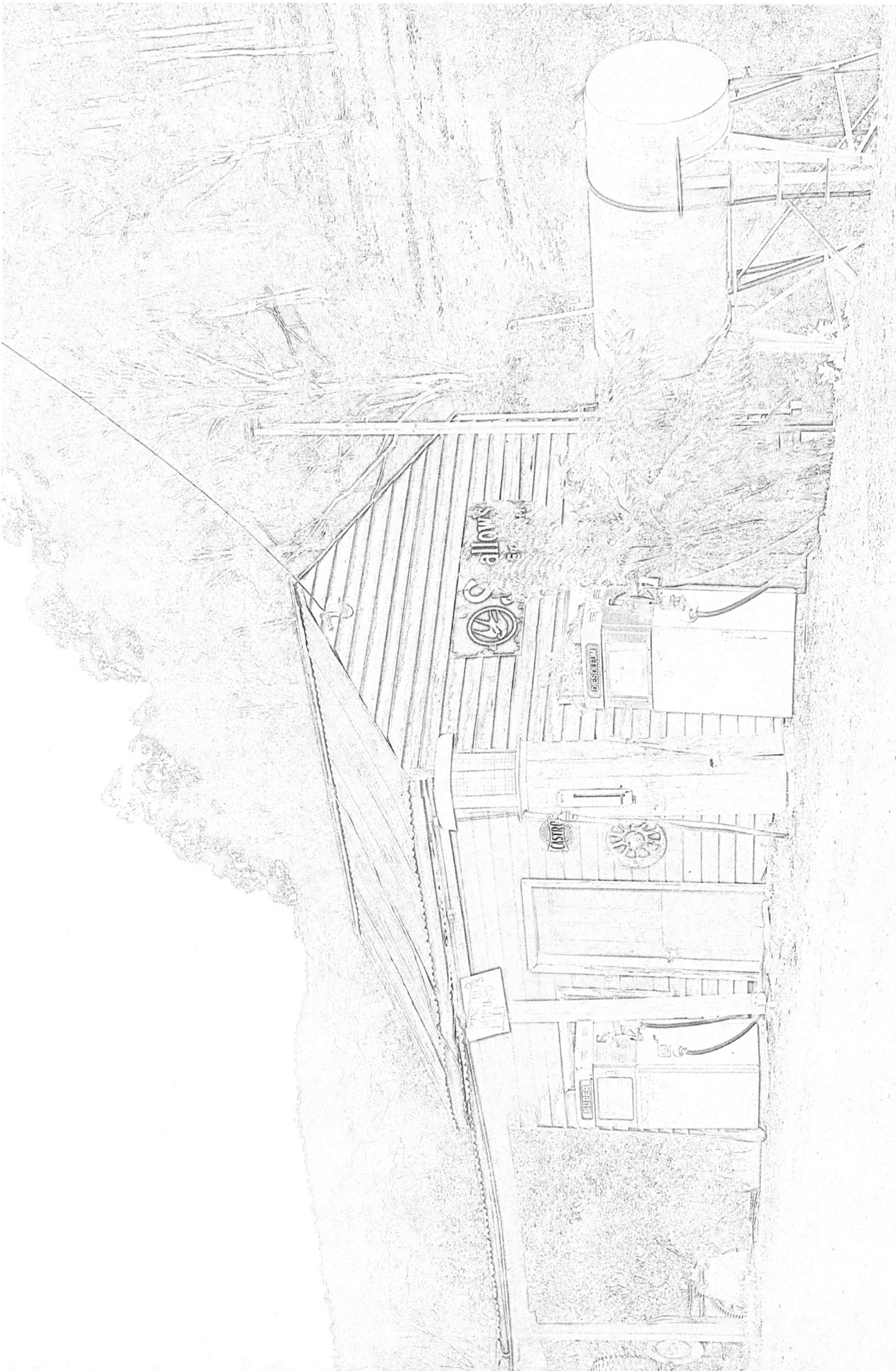
DIESEL
SUPER

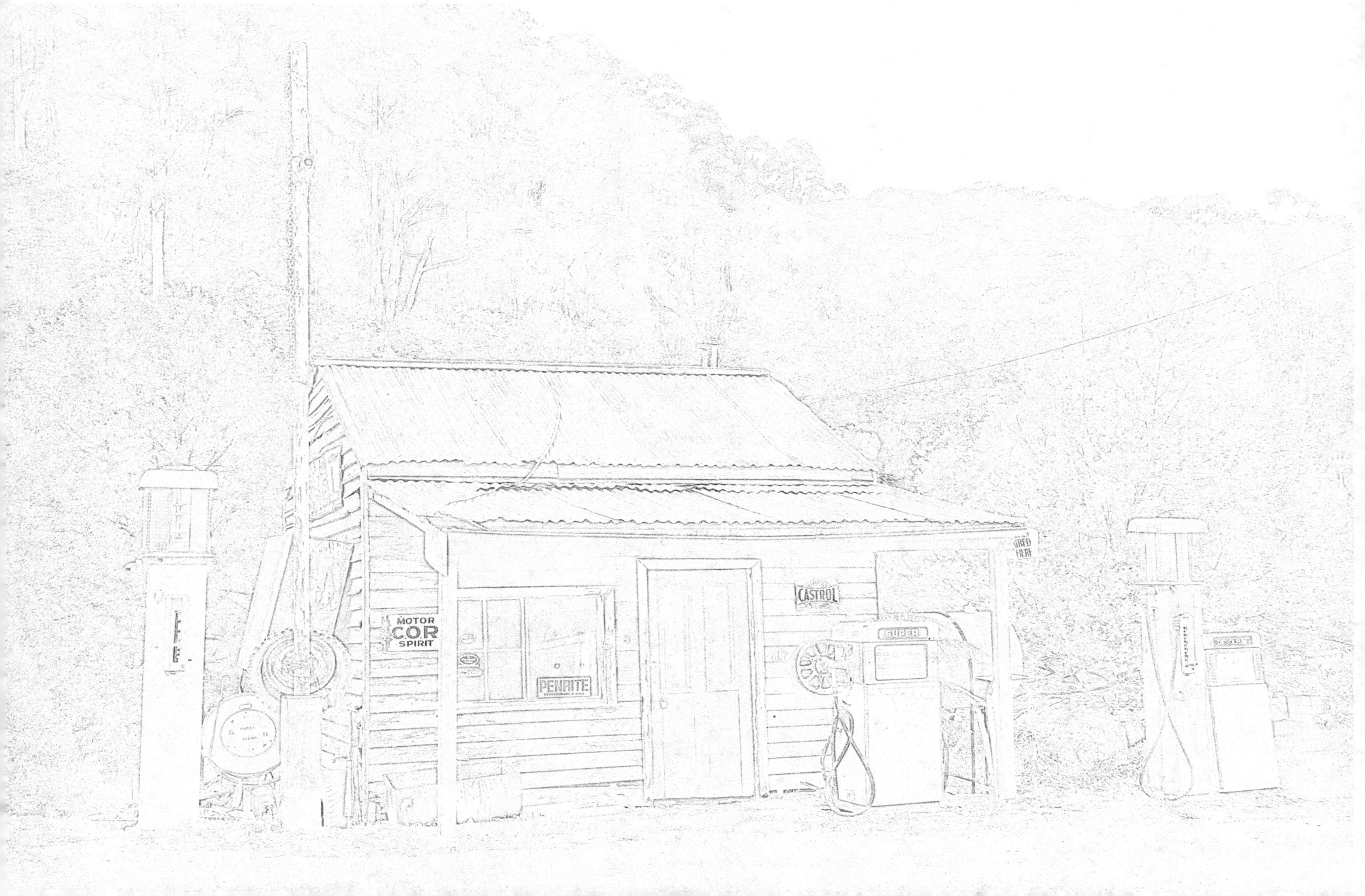
MOTOR
COR
SPIRIT
PENRITE
CASTROL
SUPER

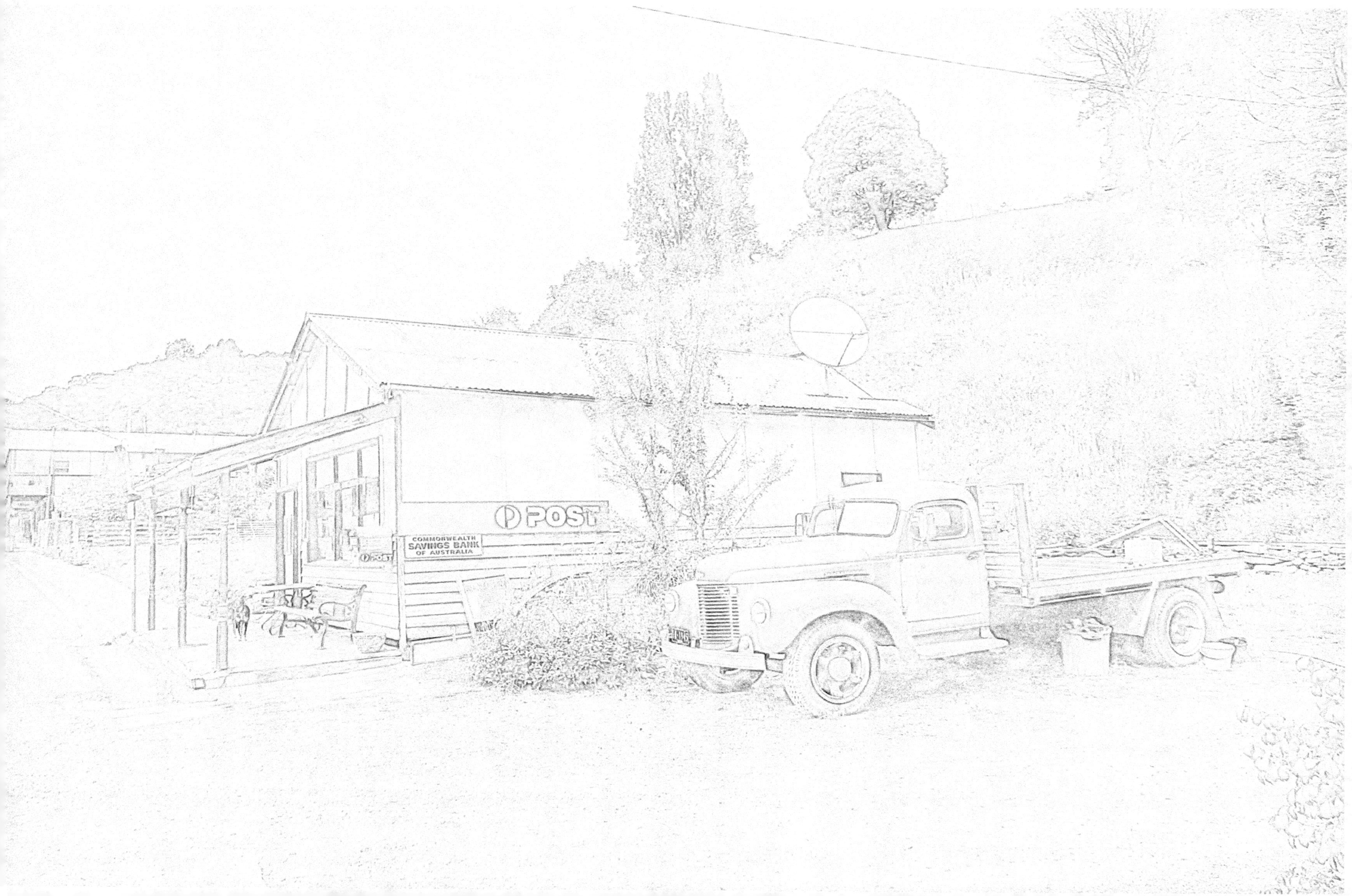
POST
COMMONWEALTH
SAVINGS BANK
OF AUSTRALIA

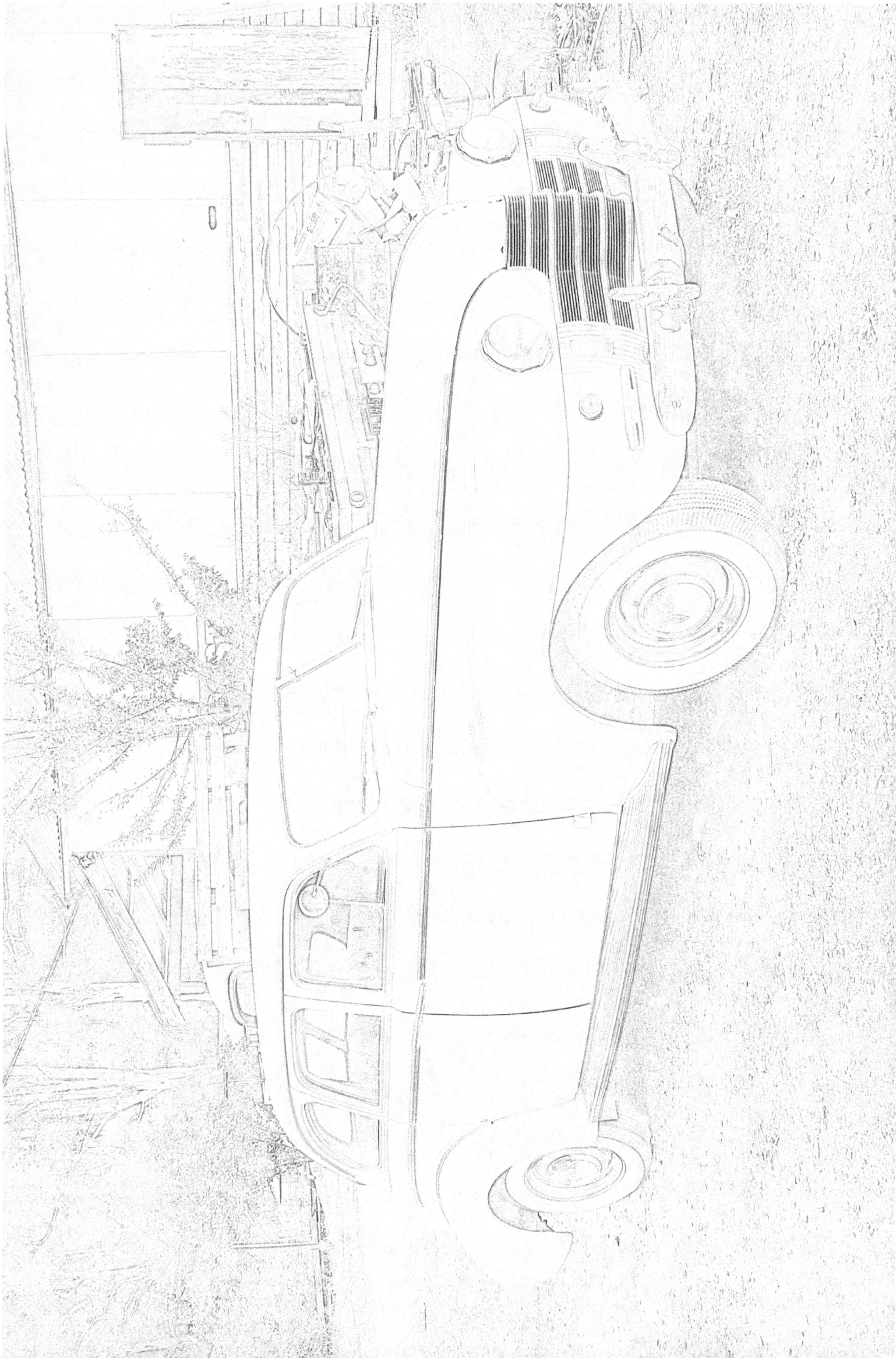

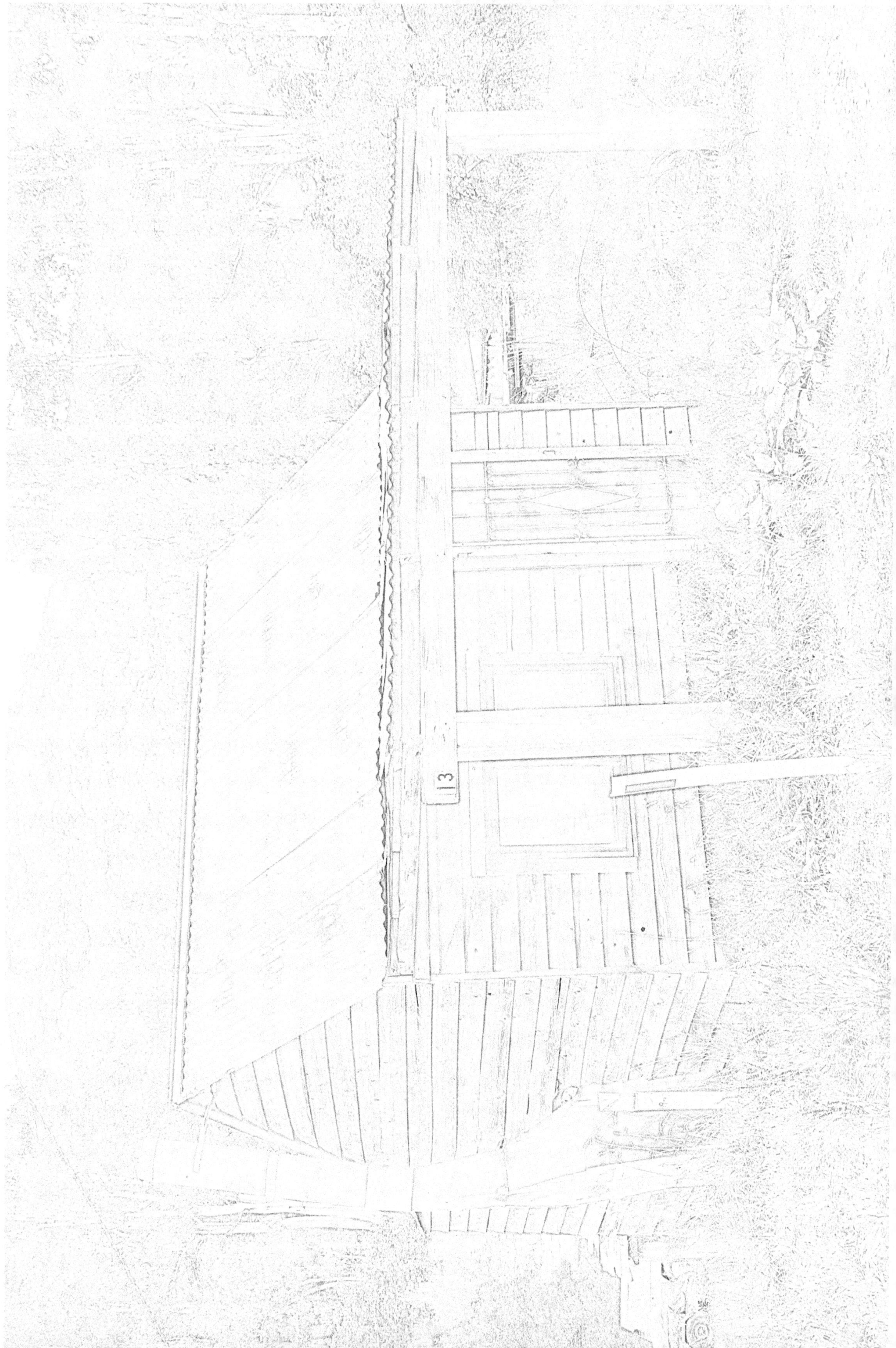
13

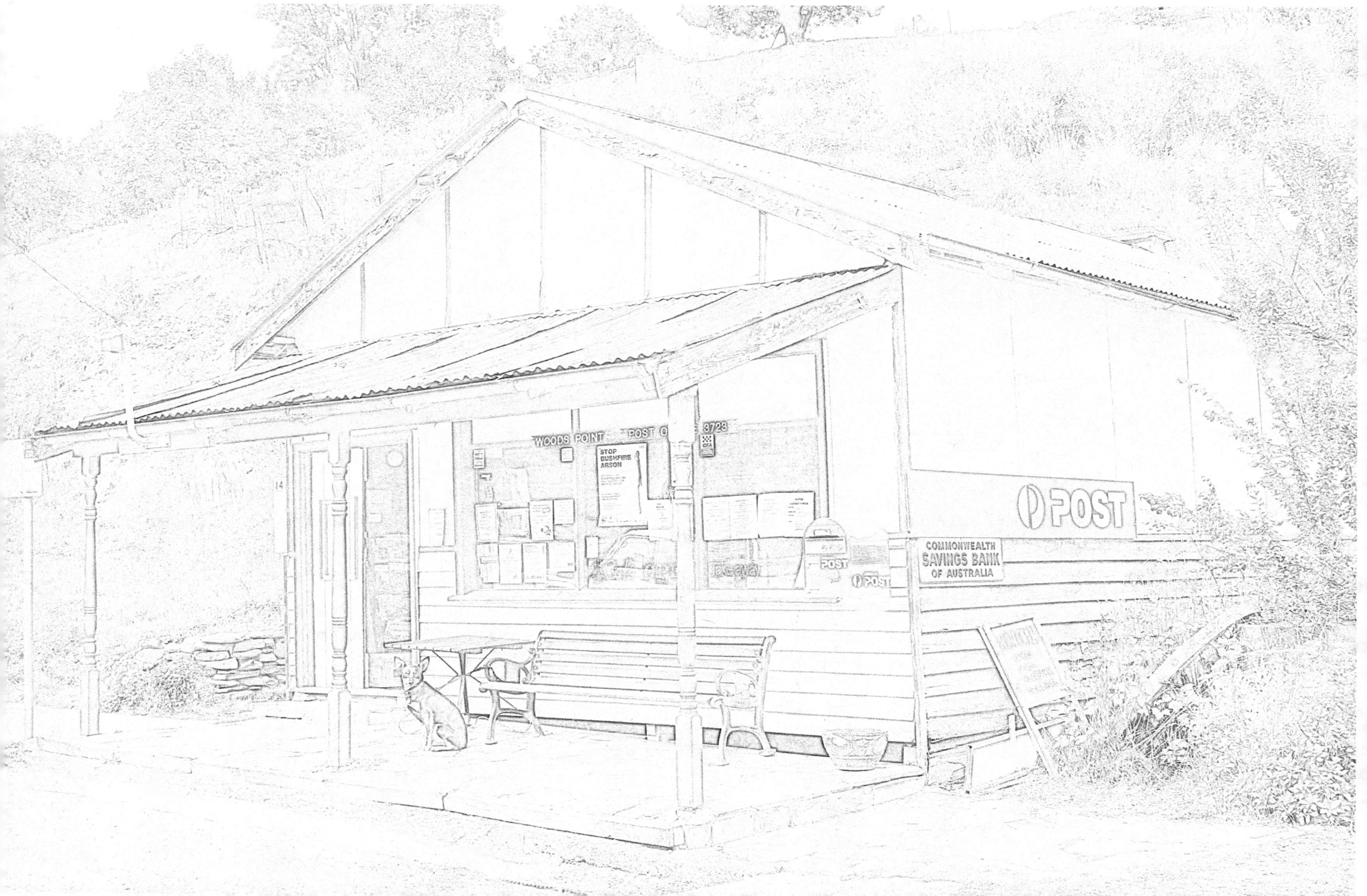
WOODS POINT
POST O
3728
STOP
BUSHFIRE
ARSON
POST
COMMONWEALTH
SAVINGS BANK
OF AUSTRALIA
POST
POST

Community Bank Branch
Bendigo Bank

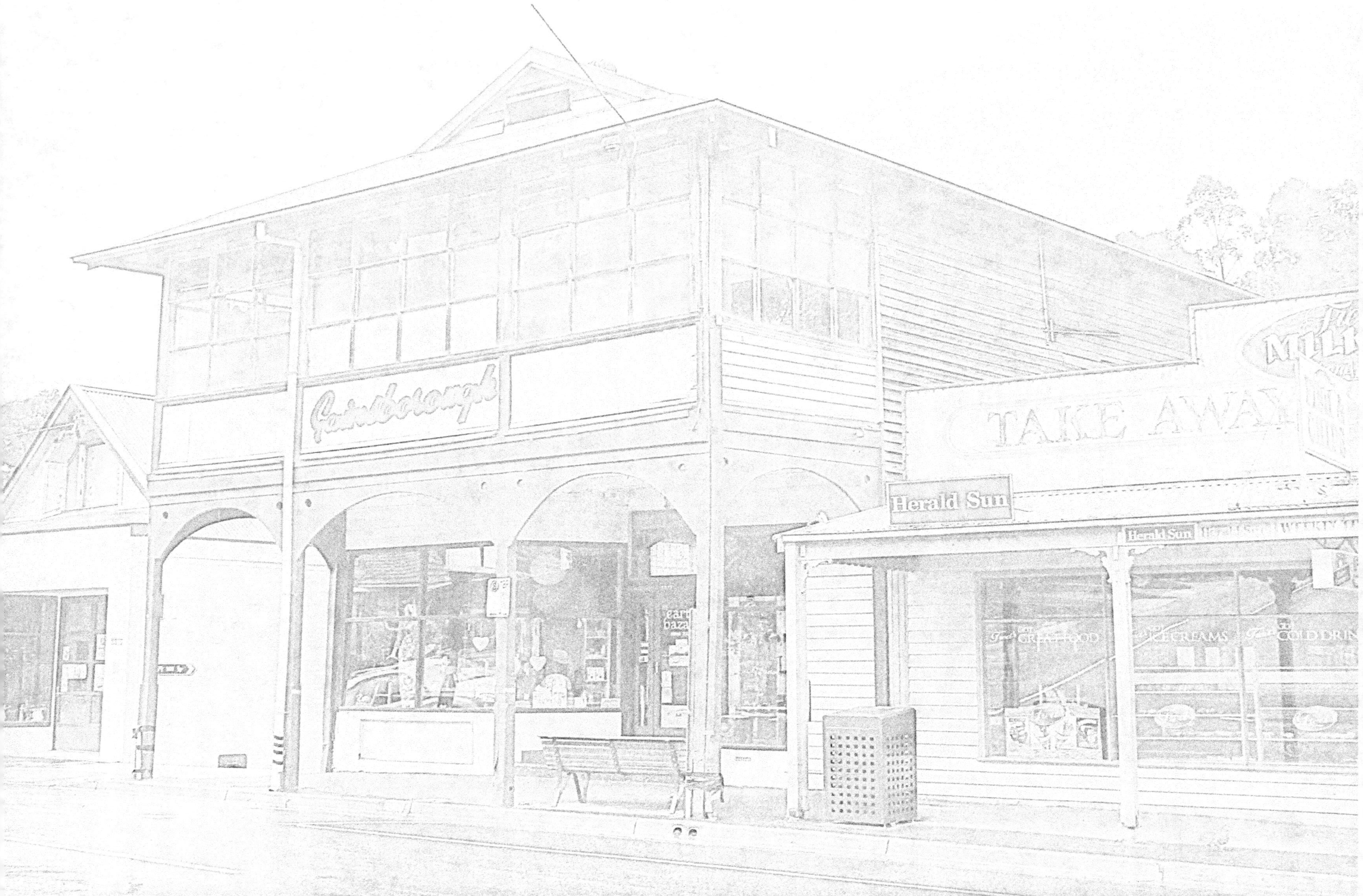
Herald Sun
TAKE AWAY
Herald Sun
GREENGROCERY
ICECREAMS
COLD DRINKS

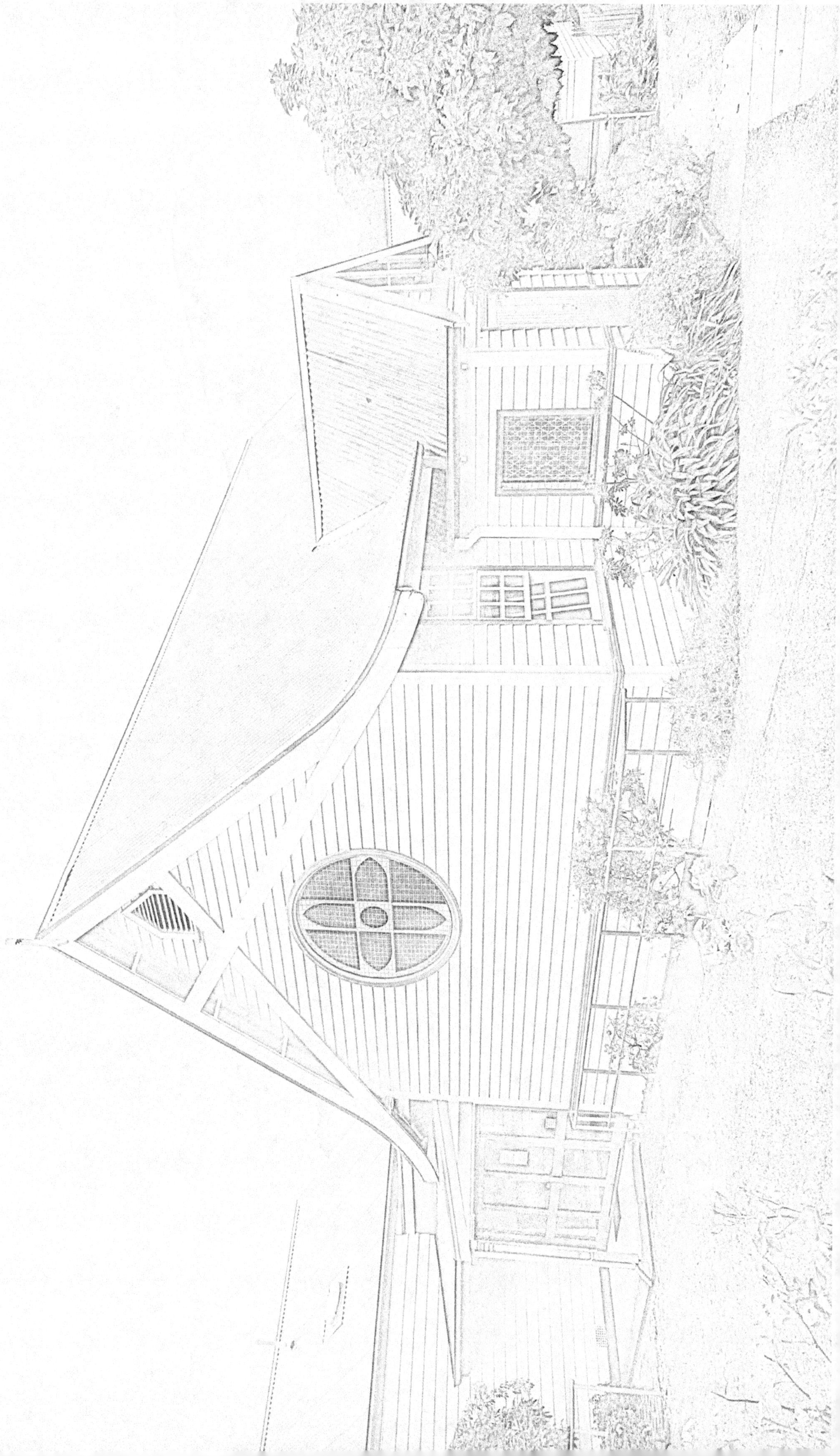

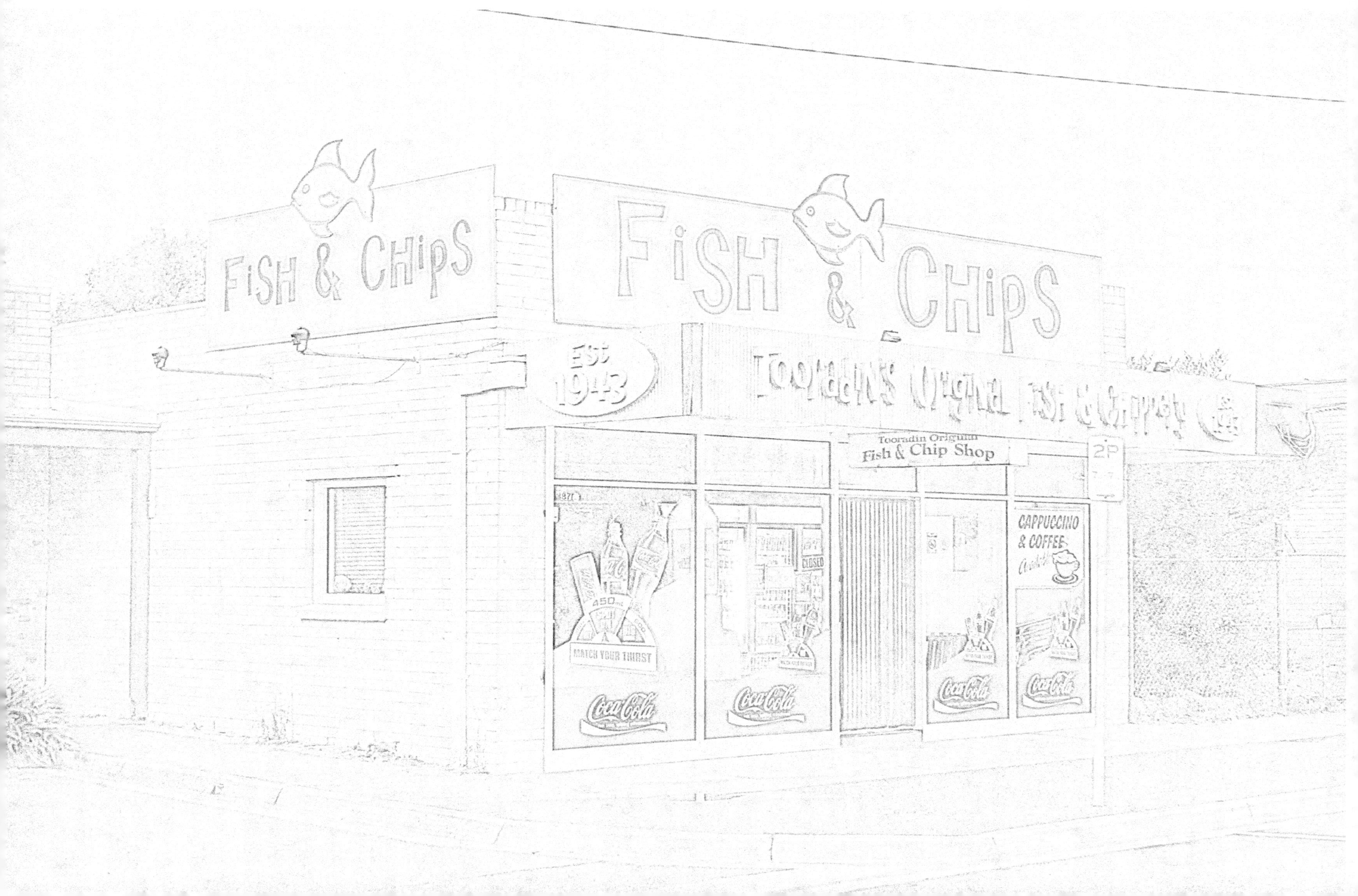
FISH & CHIPS
FISH & CHIPS
Est 1943
Tooradin Original
Fish & Chip Shop
2P
CLOSED
CAPPUCCINO
& COFFEE
450ml
MATCH YOUR THIRST
Coca-Cola
Coca-Cola
Coca-Cola
Coca-Cola

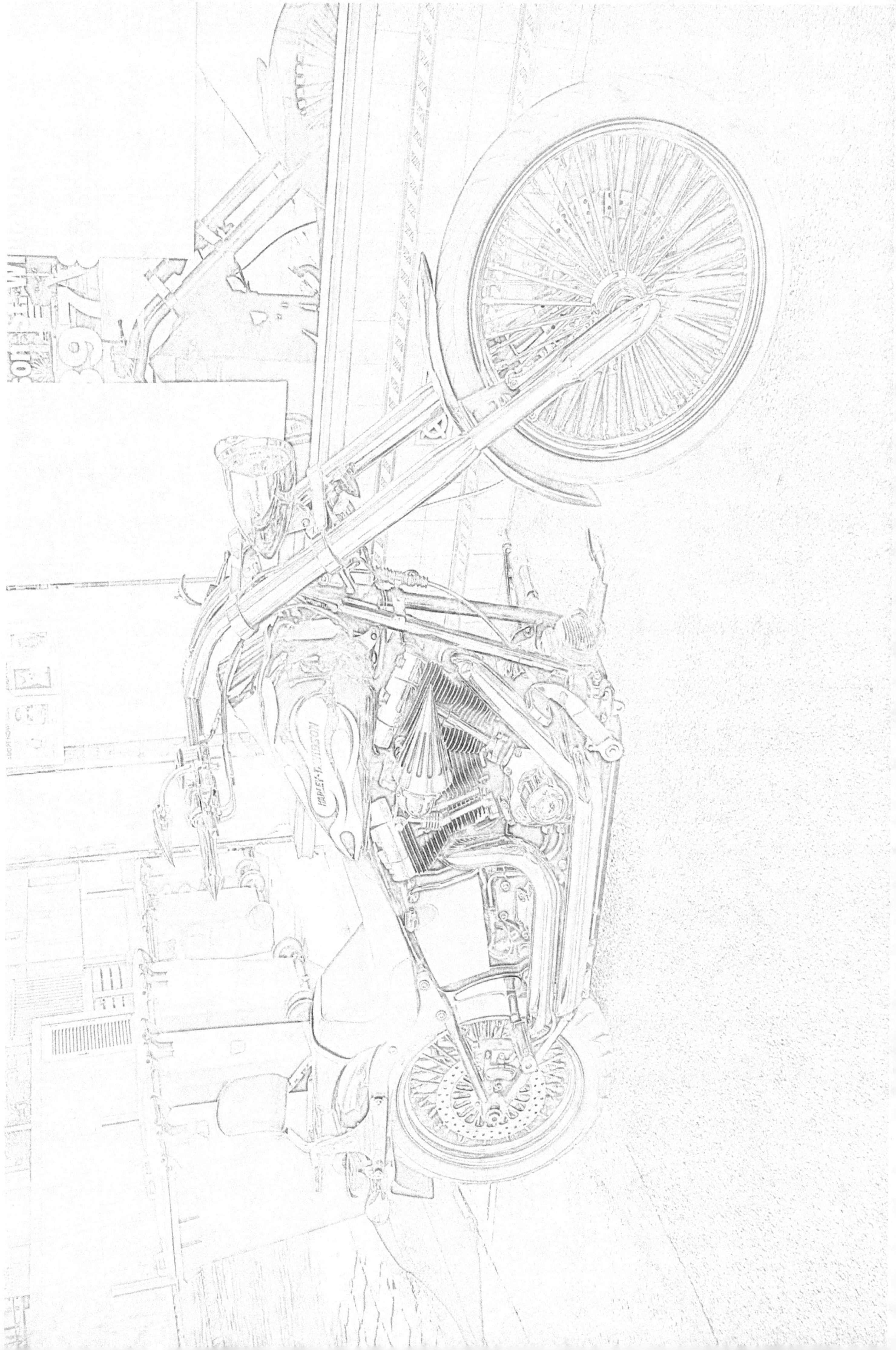
HARLEY-DAVIDSON

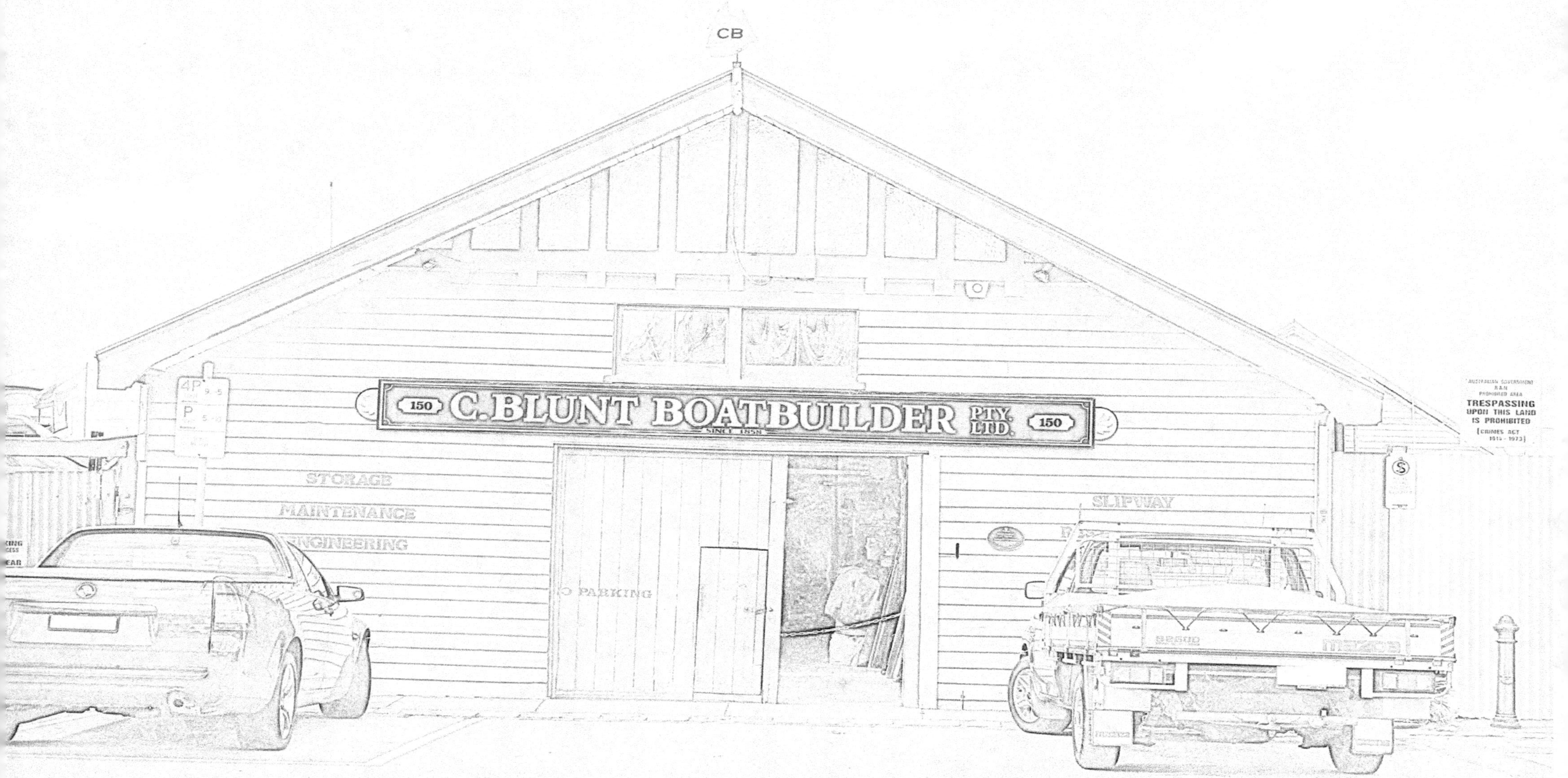
CB
150
C. BLUNT BOATBUILDER PTY. LTD.
SINCE 1858
150
STORAGE
MAINTENANCE
ENGINEERING
PARKING
SLIPWAY
TRESPASSING
UPON THIS LAND
IS PROHIBITED

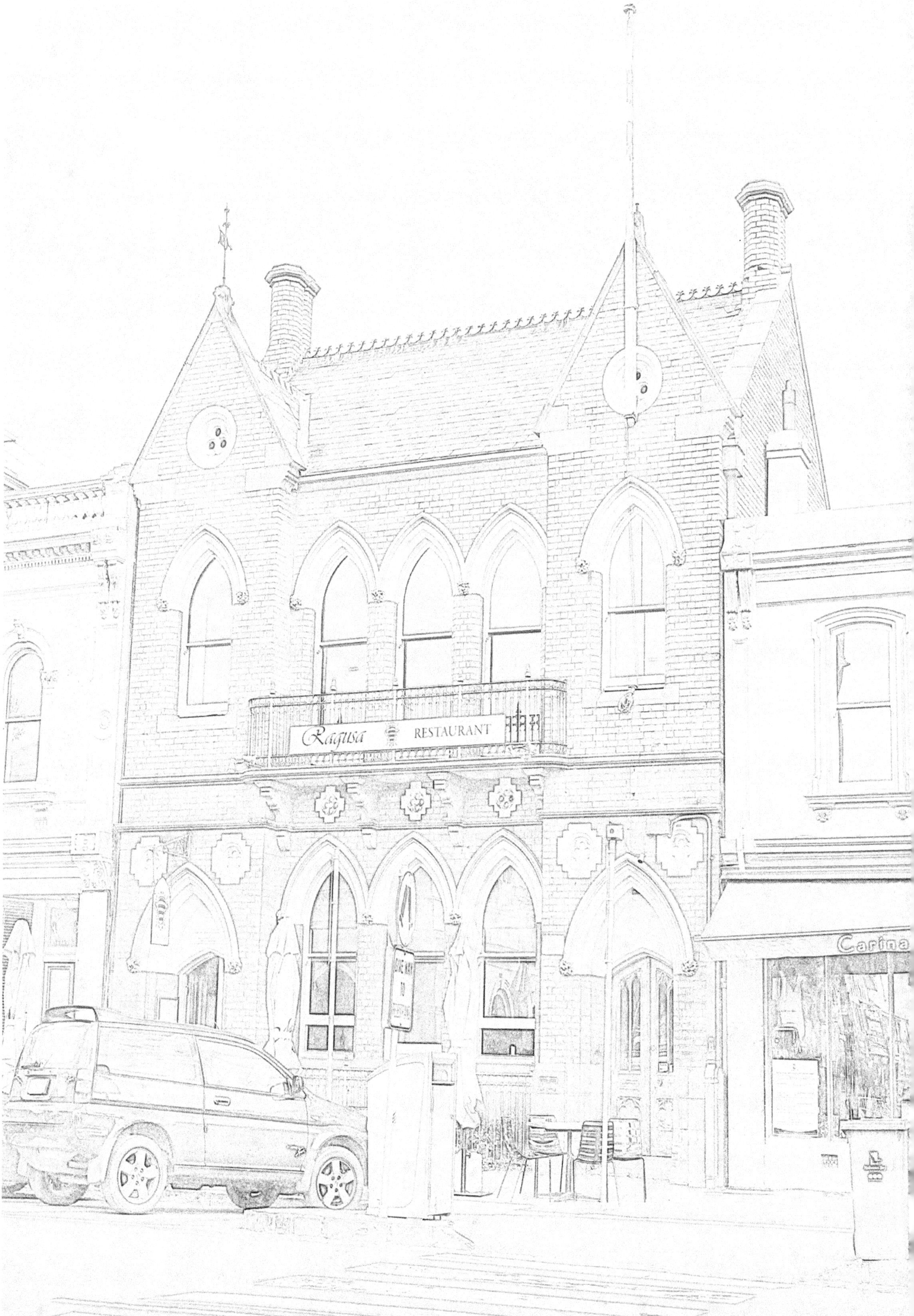

Ragusa RESTAURANT
Carina

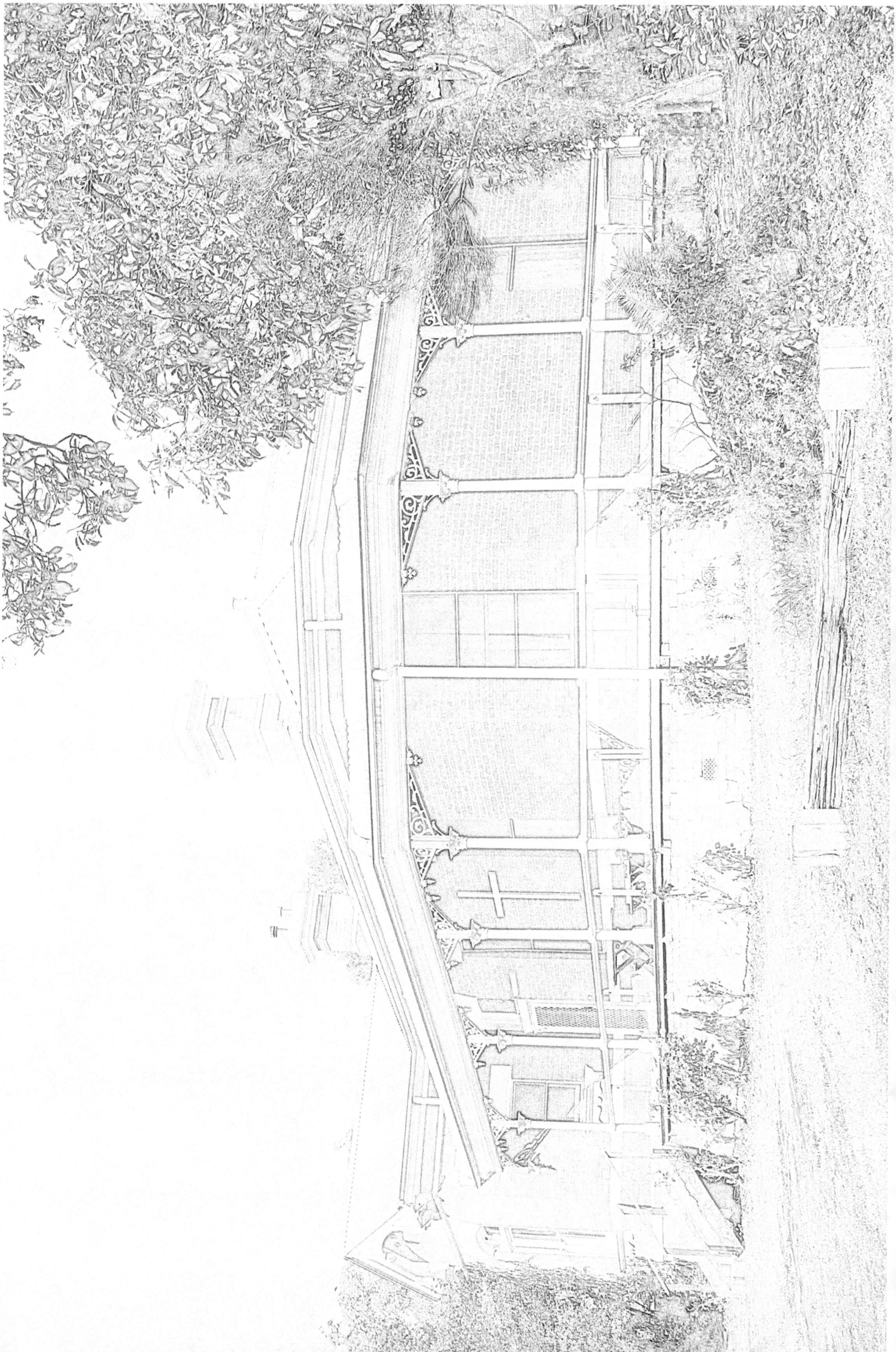

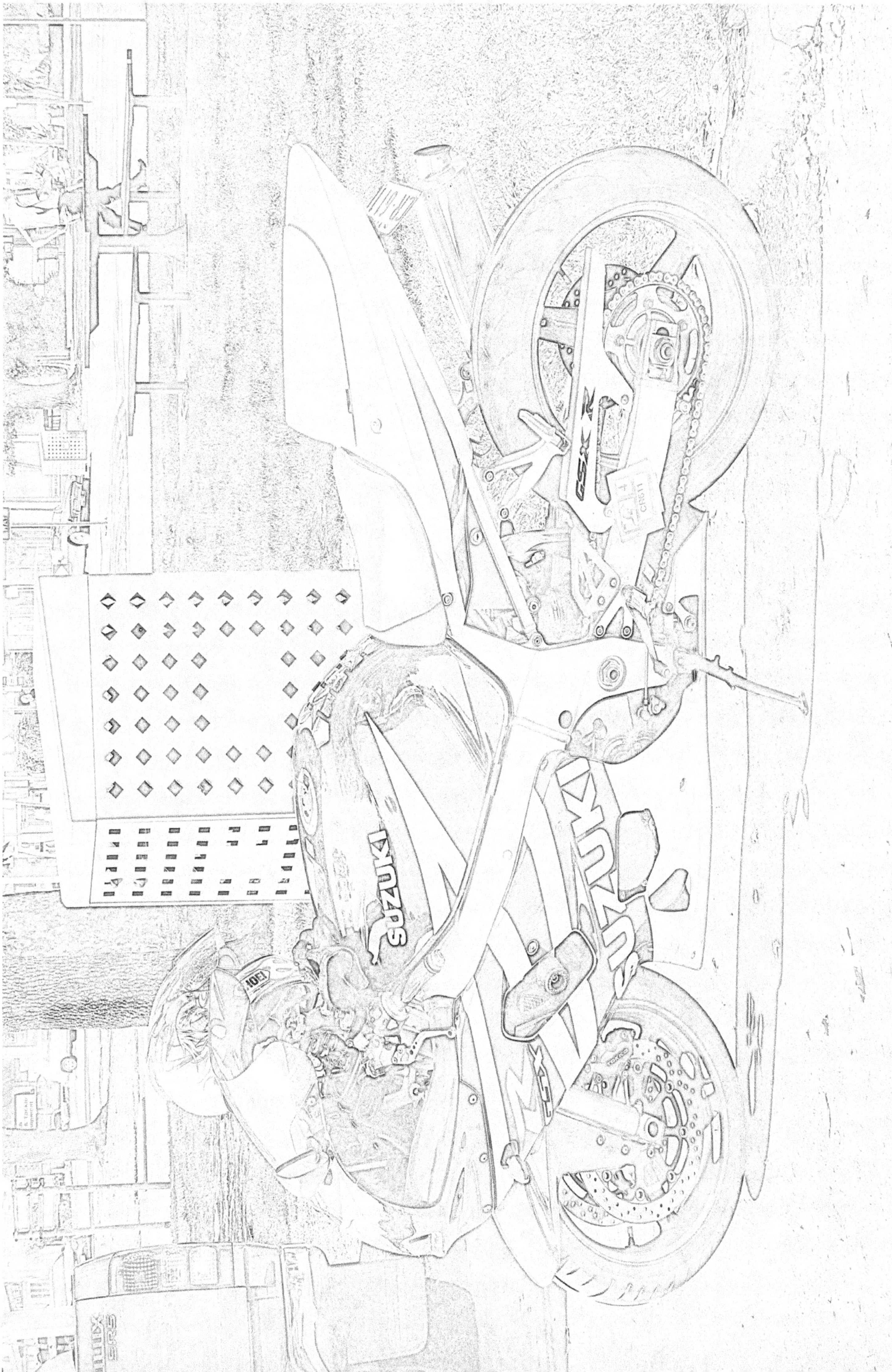
SUZUKI
SUZUKI

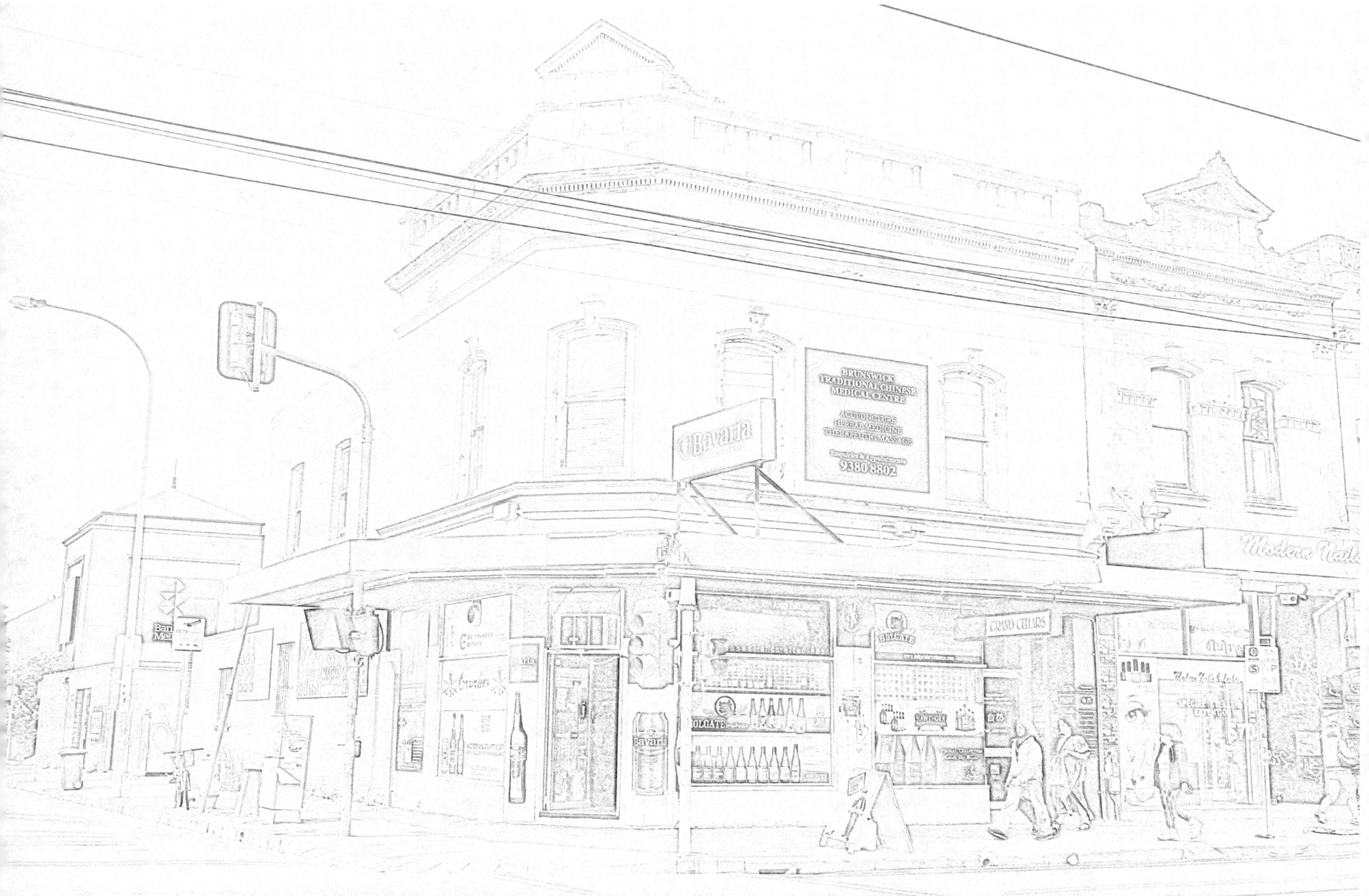
BRUNSWICK
TRADITIONAL CHINESE
MEDICAL CENTRE
ACUPUNCTURE
HERBAL MEDICINE
THERAPEUTIC MASSAGE
Enquiries & Appointments
9380 8802
Bavaria
GRAND CELLARS
HOLGATE
Modern Nails

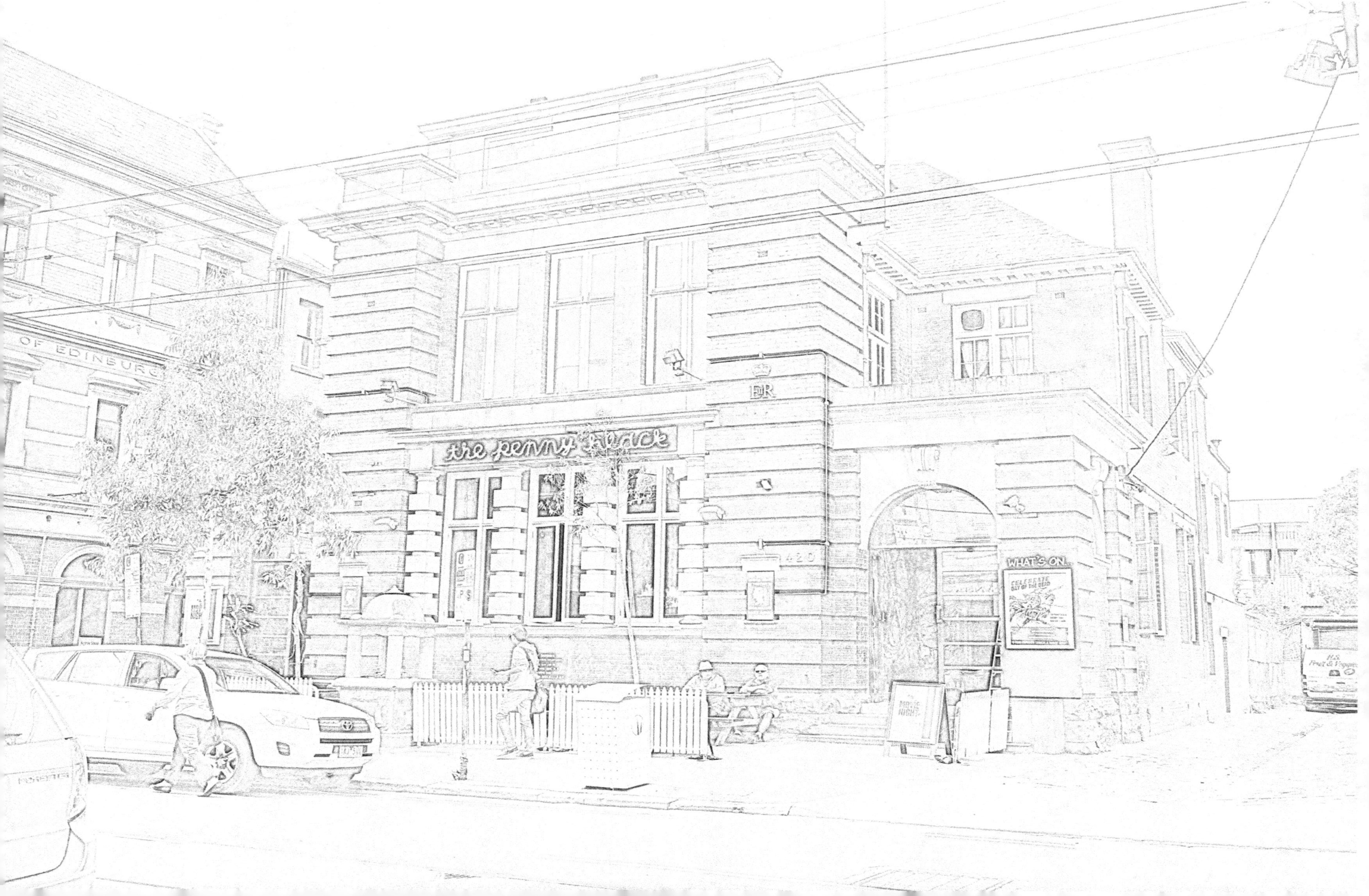
OF EDINBURG
the penny black
ER
420
WHAT'S ON
CELEBRATE DAY OF THE DEAD

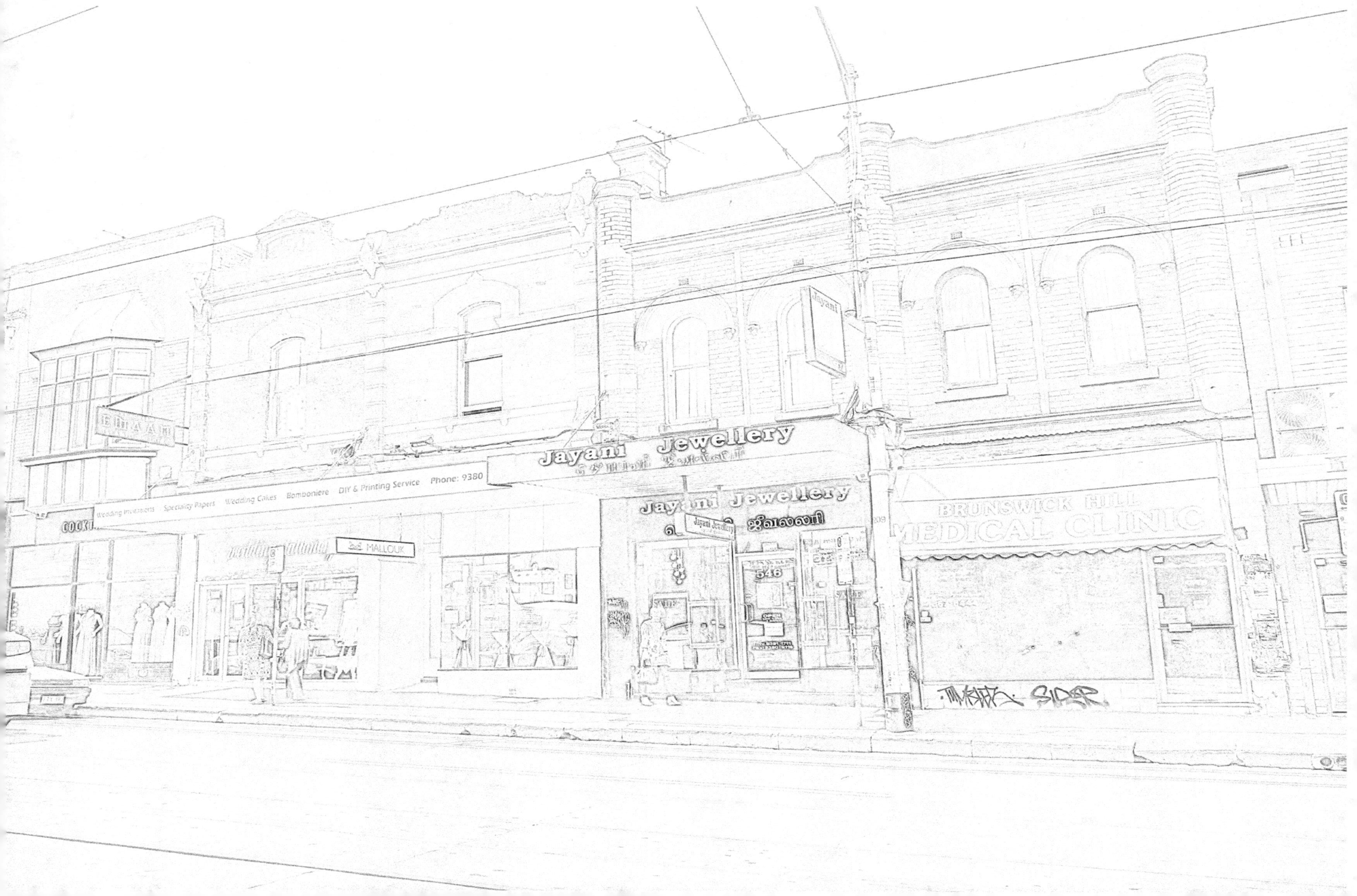

Jayani Jewellery
Wedding Invitations Speciality Papers Wedding Cakes Bomboniere DIY & Printing Service Phone: 9380
Jayani
Jayani Jewellery
ஜீவலலரி
Jayani Jewellery
546
MALLOUK
BRUNSWICK HILL
MEDICAL CLINIC

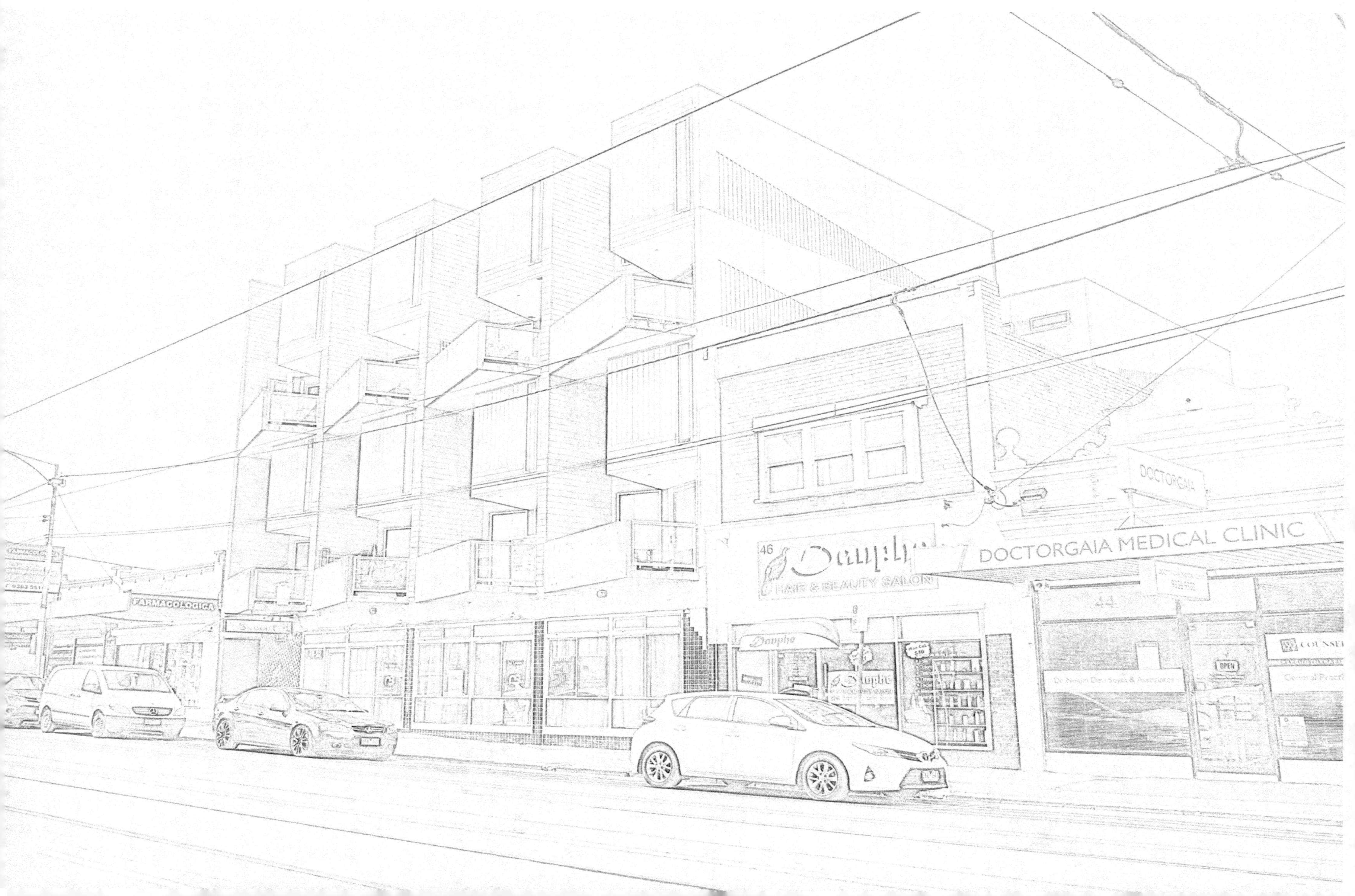
DOCTORGAIA
DOCTORGAIA MEDICAL CLINIC
46
HAIR & BEAUTY SALON
Danphe
44
OPEN
FARMACOLOGICA

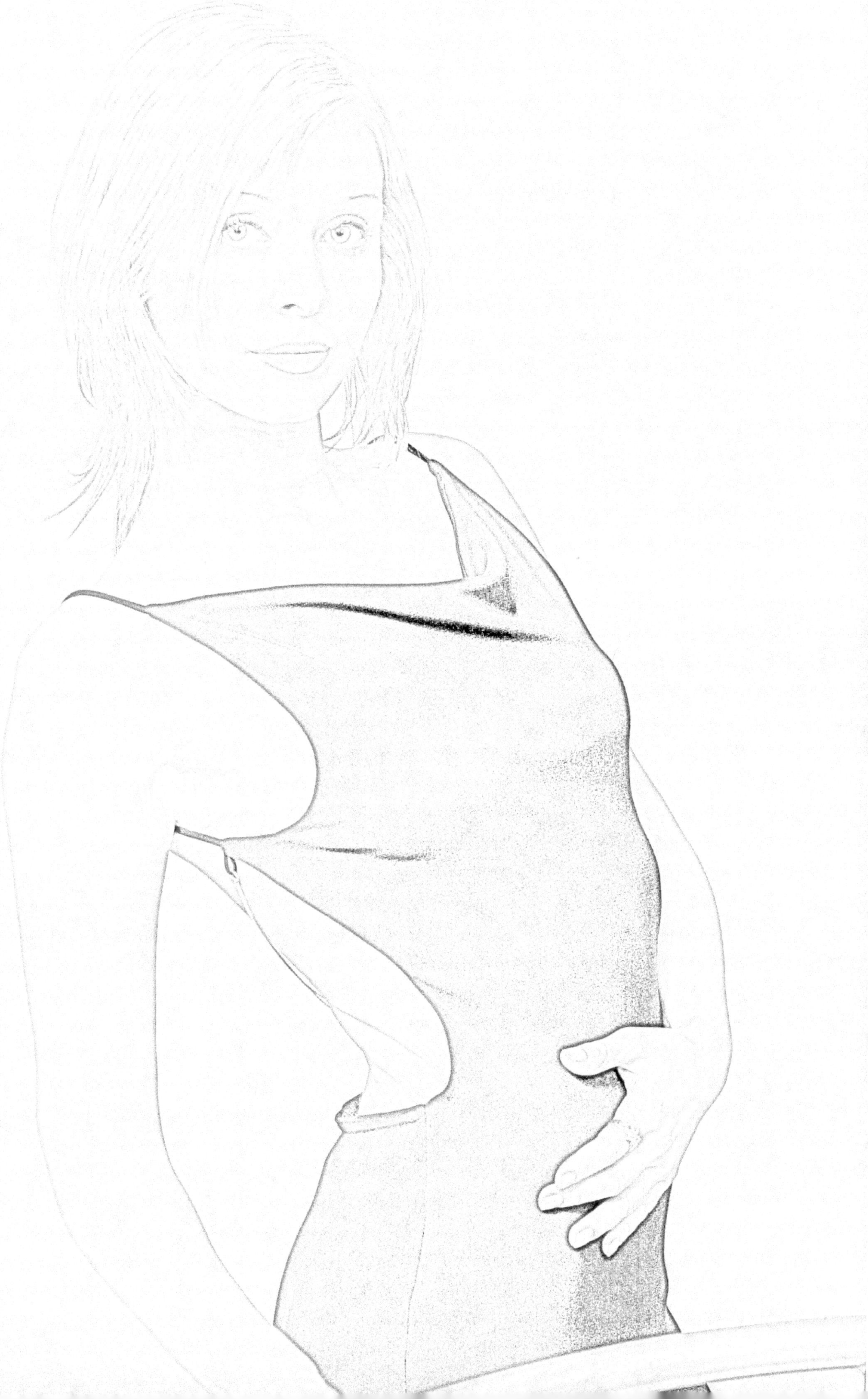

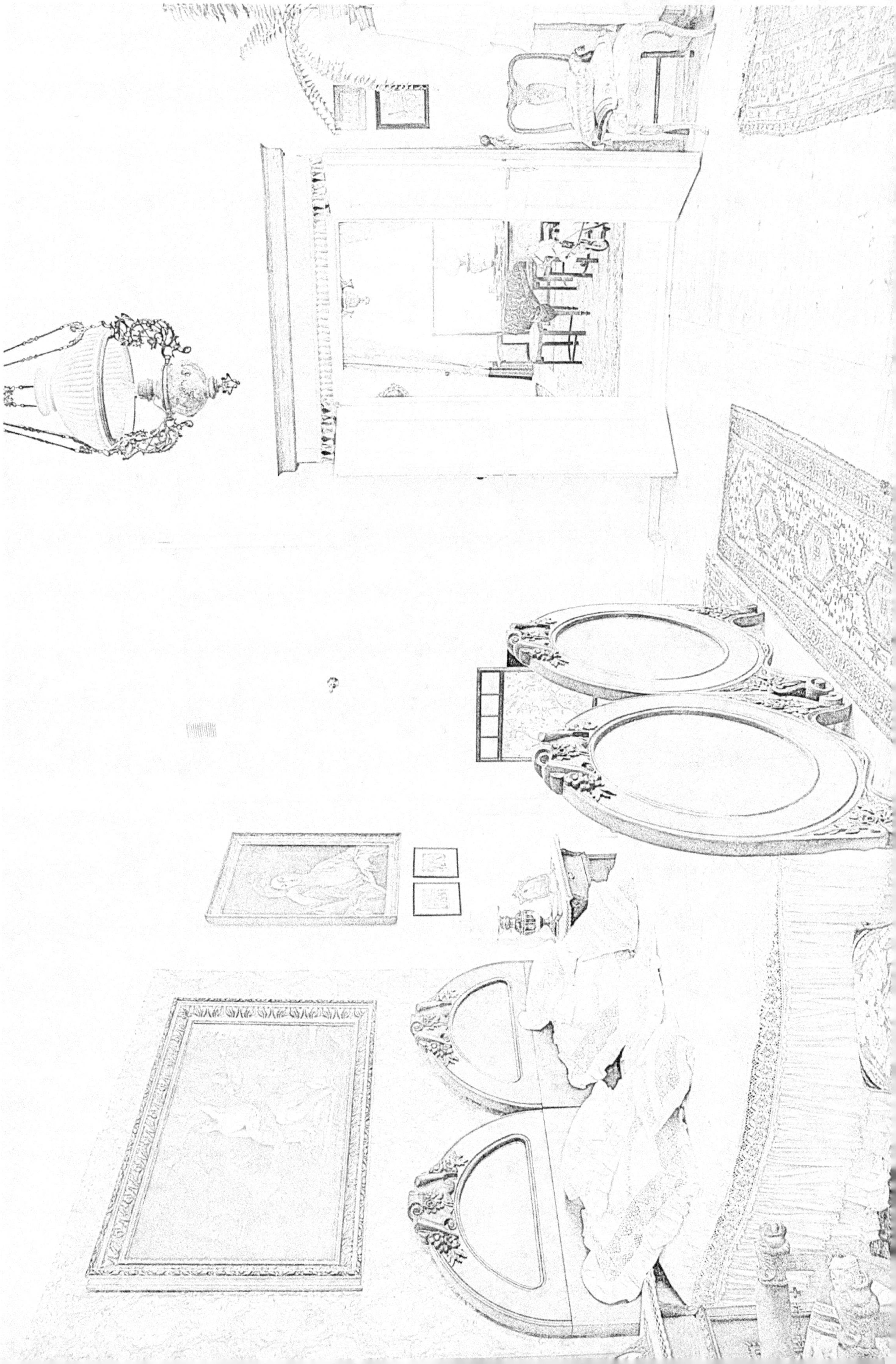

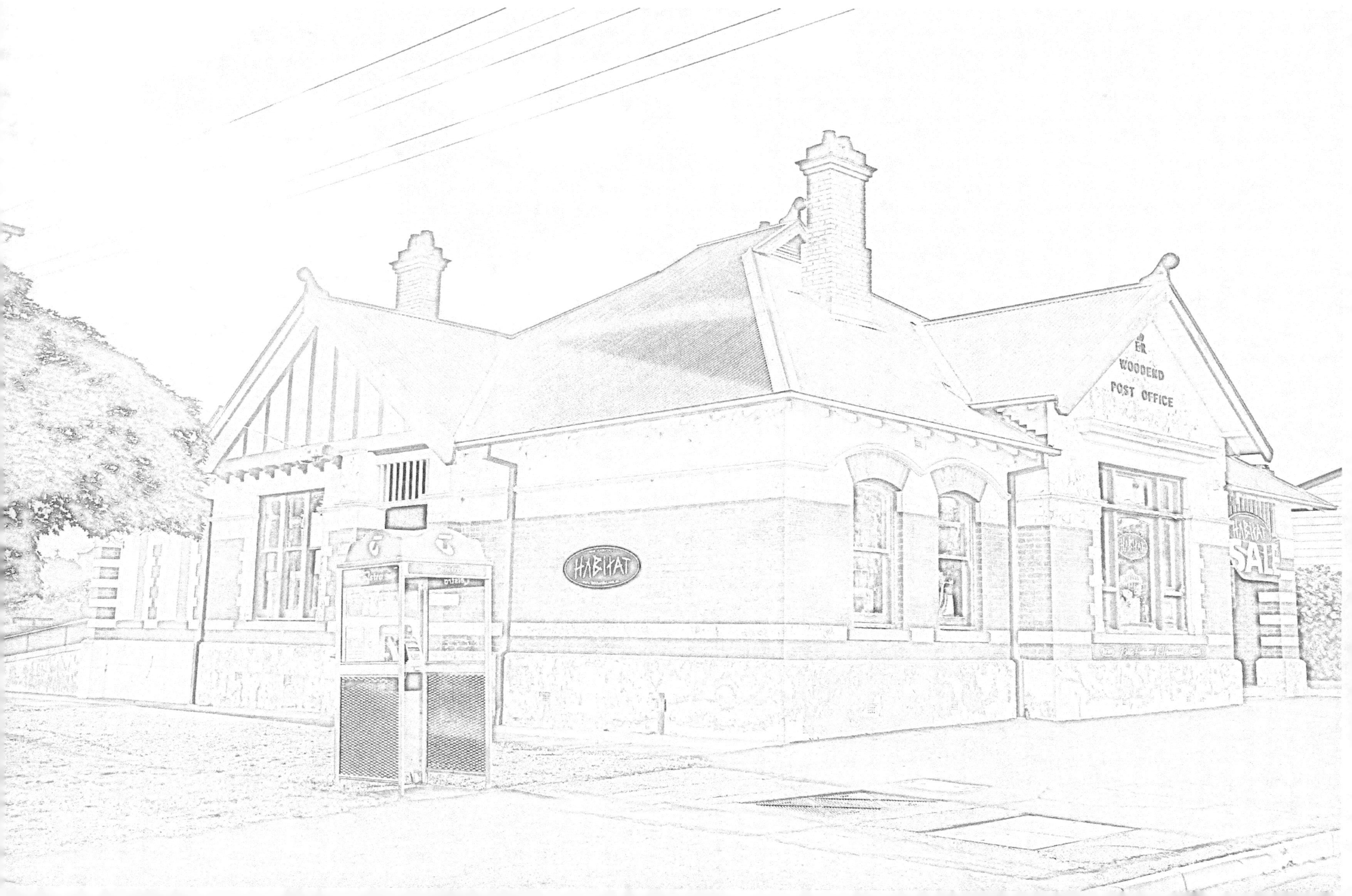
WOODEND
POST OFFICE
HABITAT
SALE

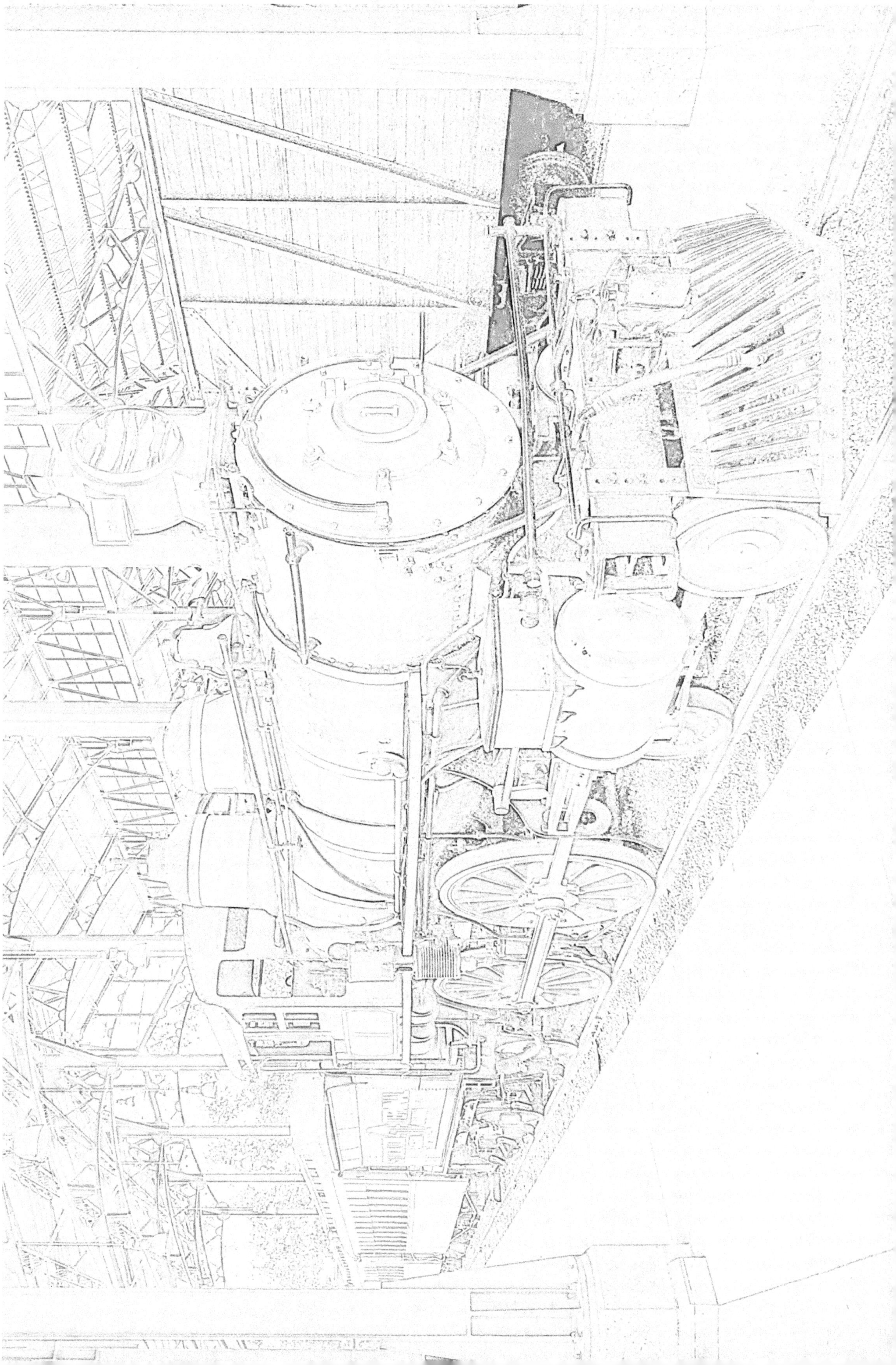

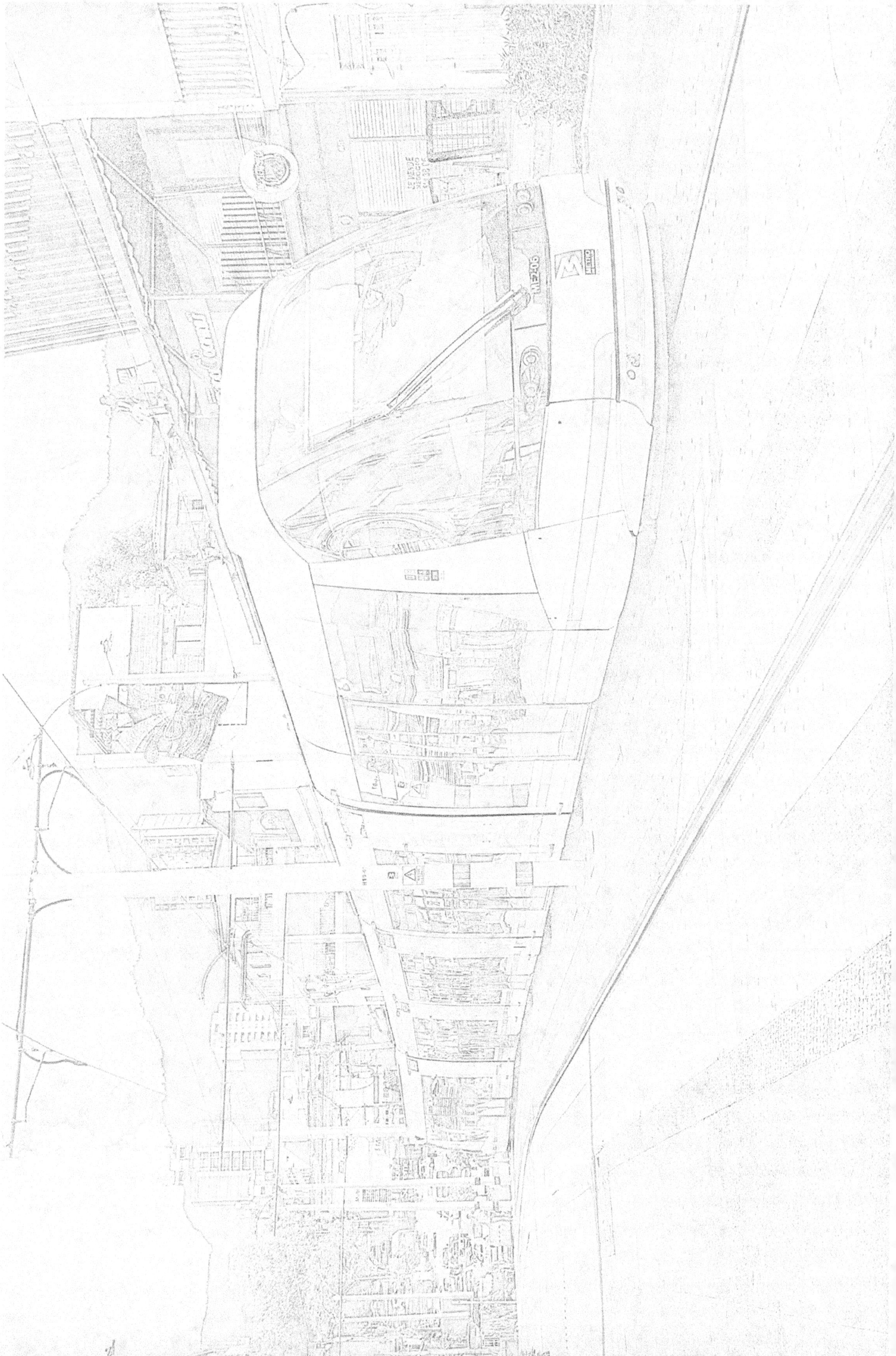

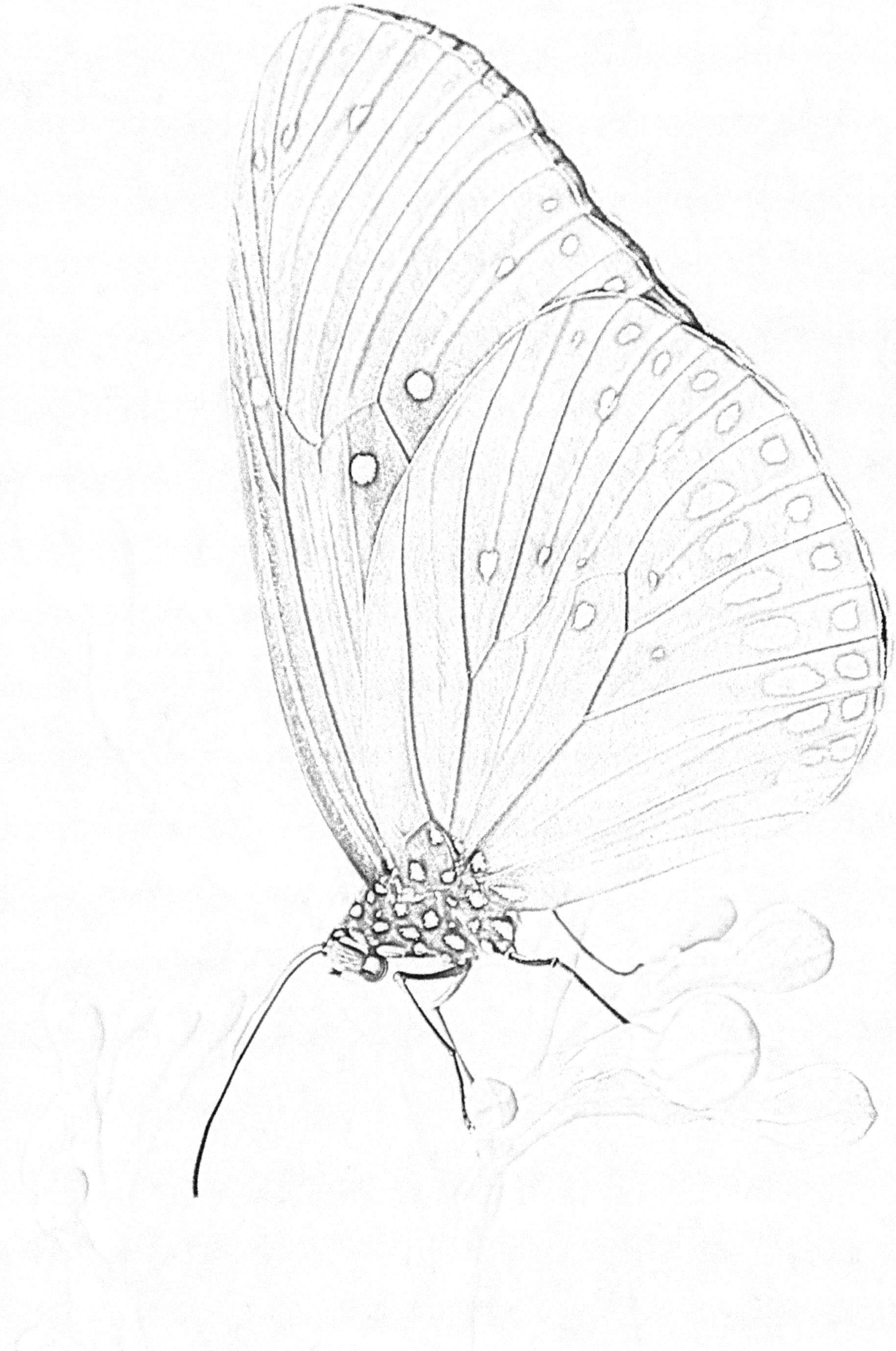

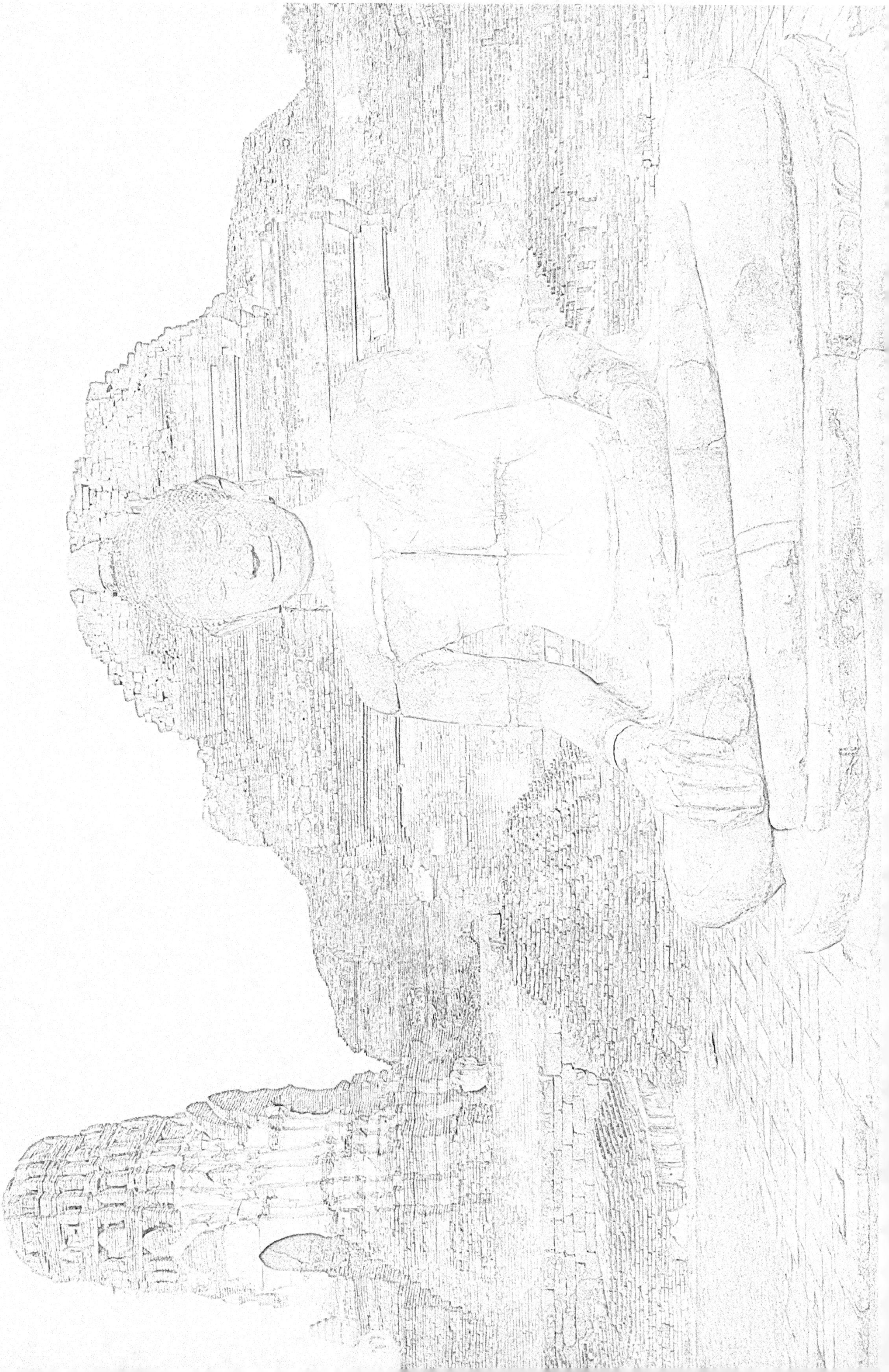

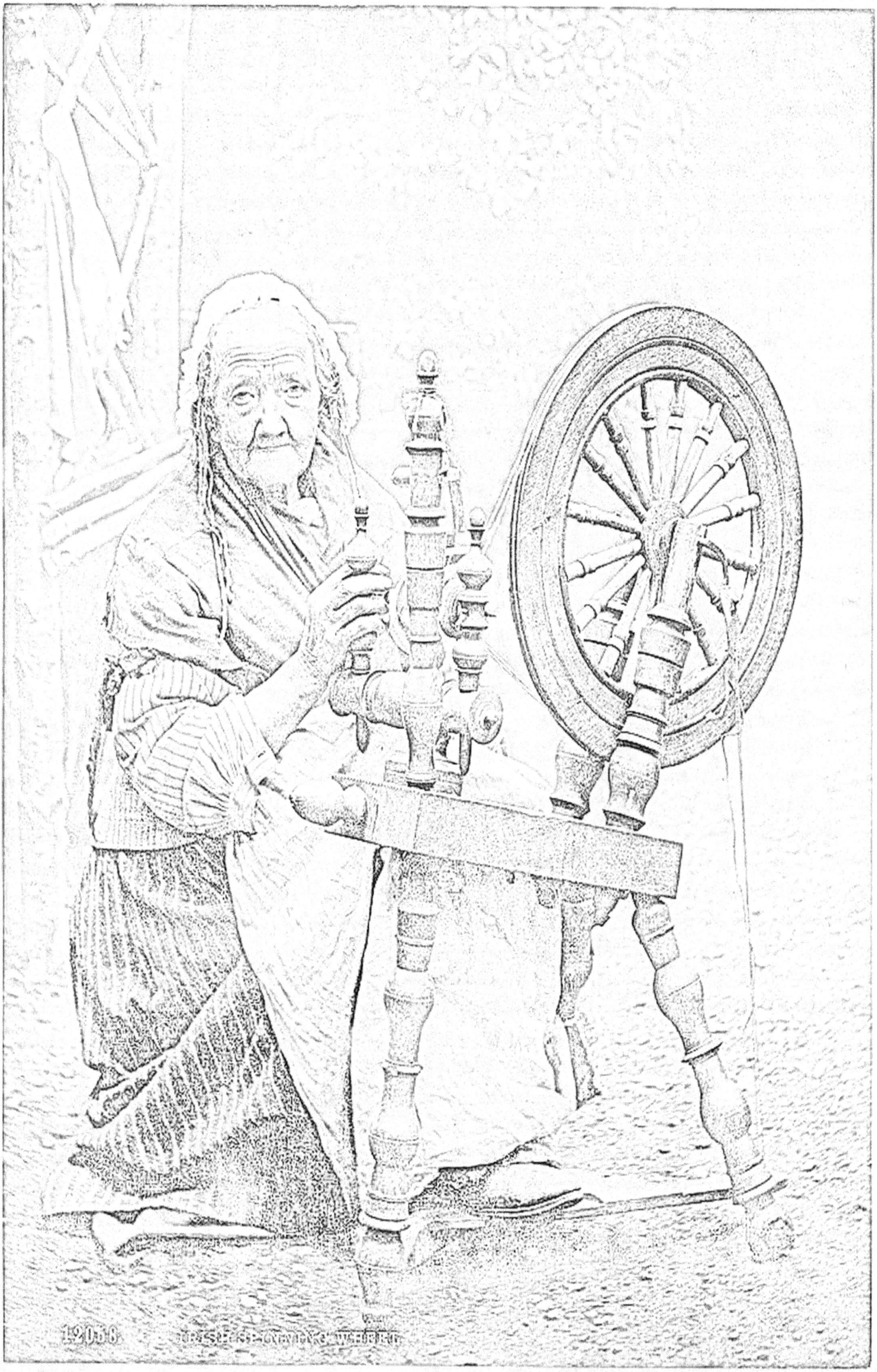
12066

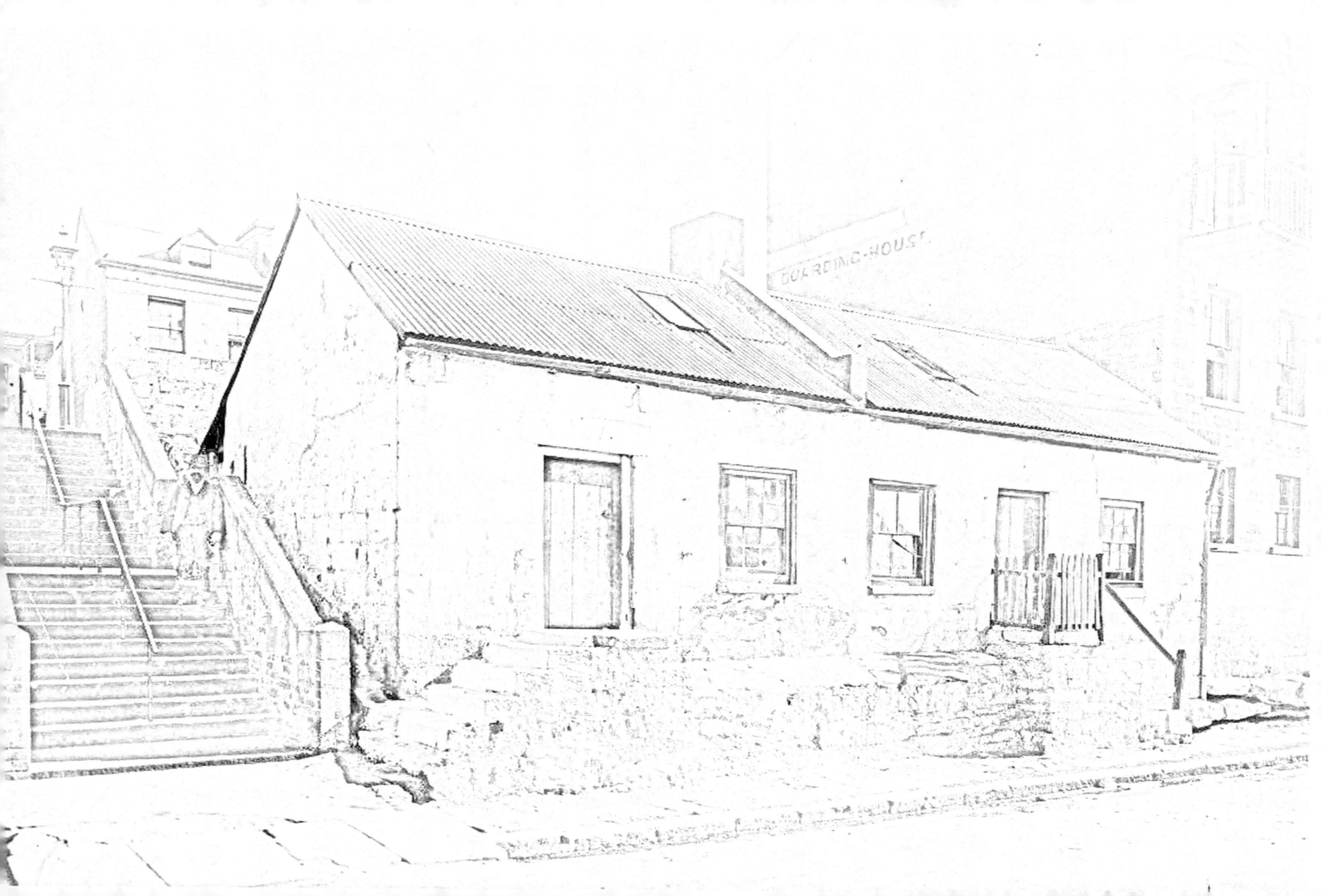

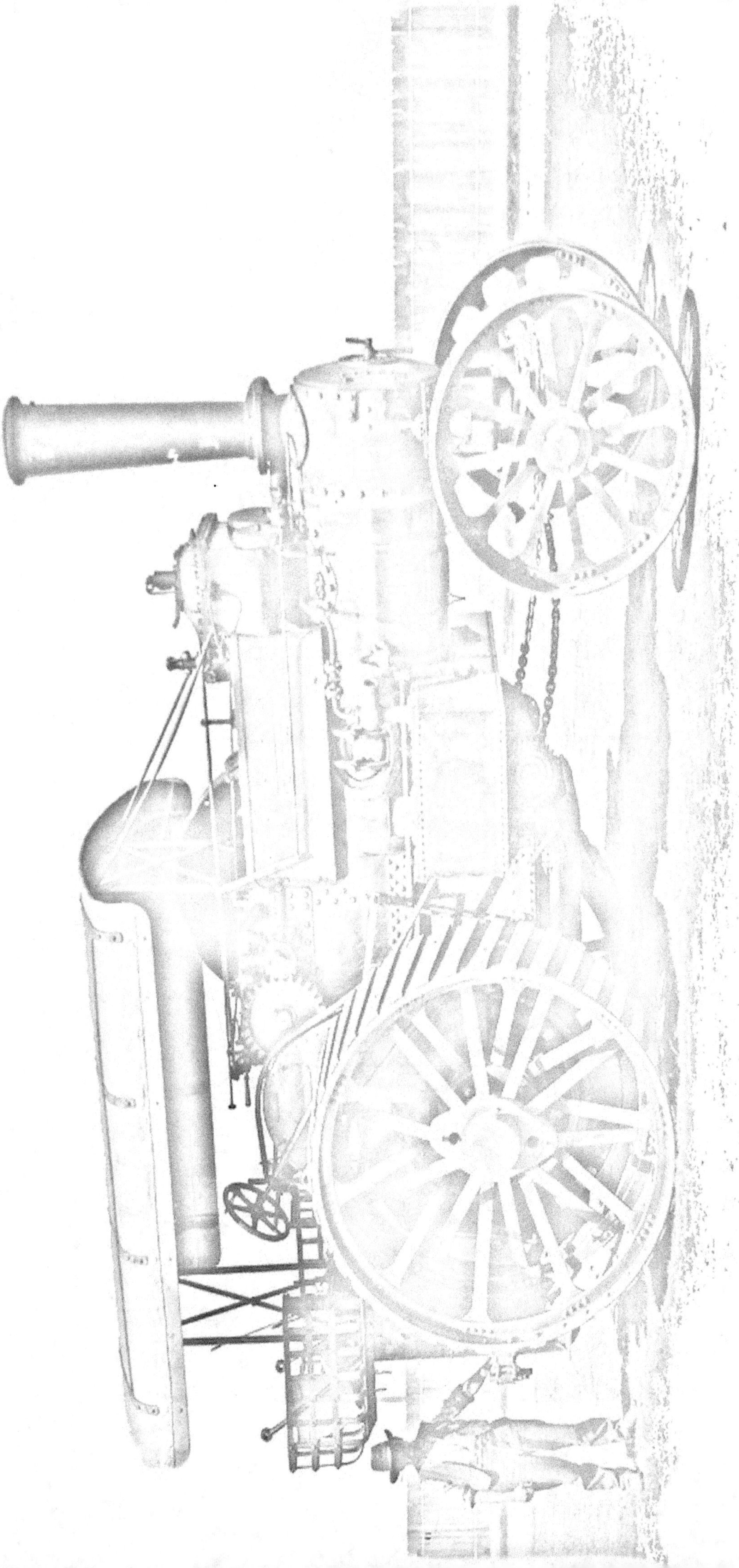

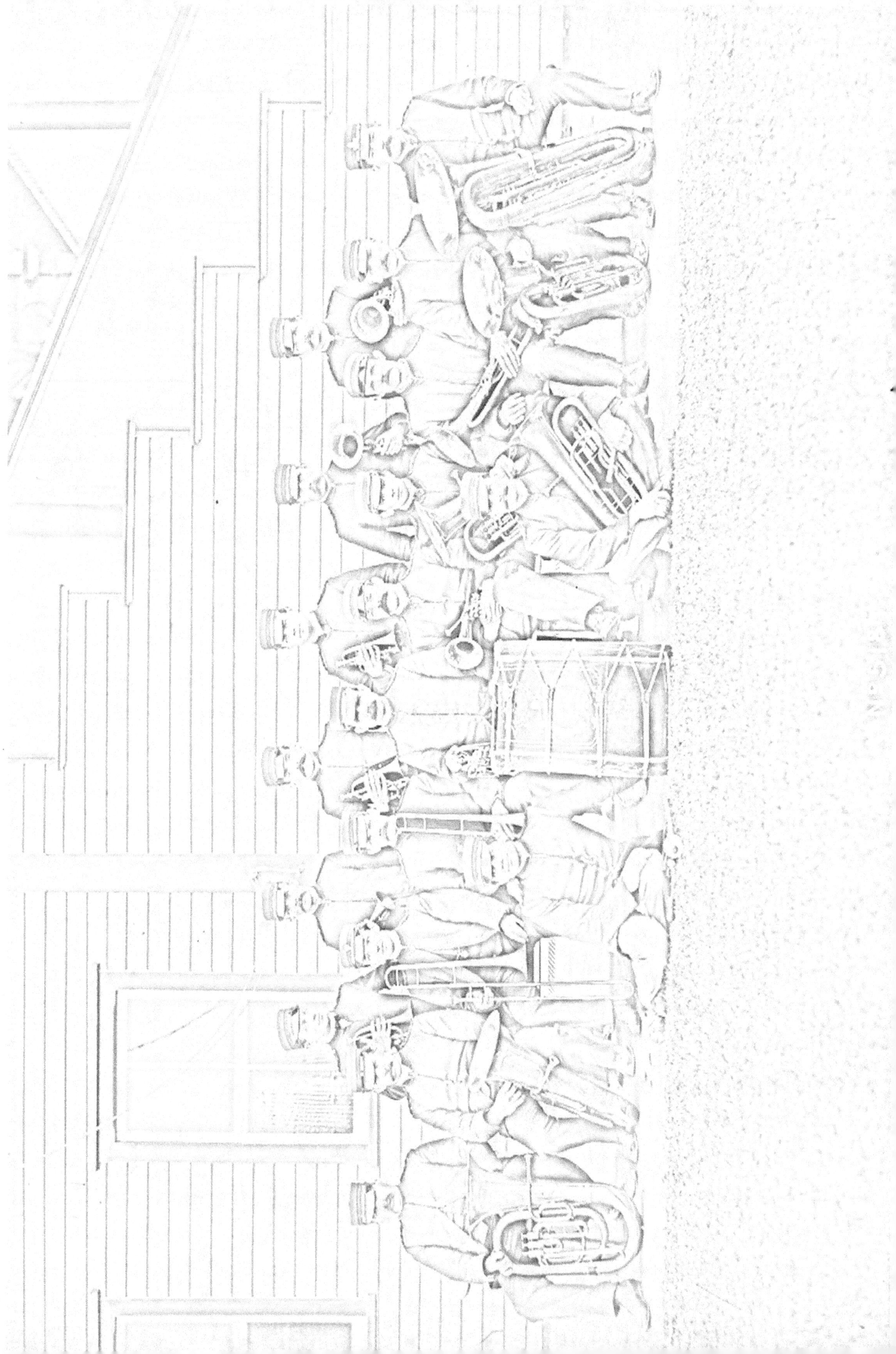

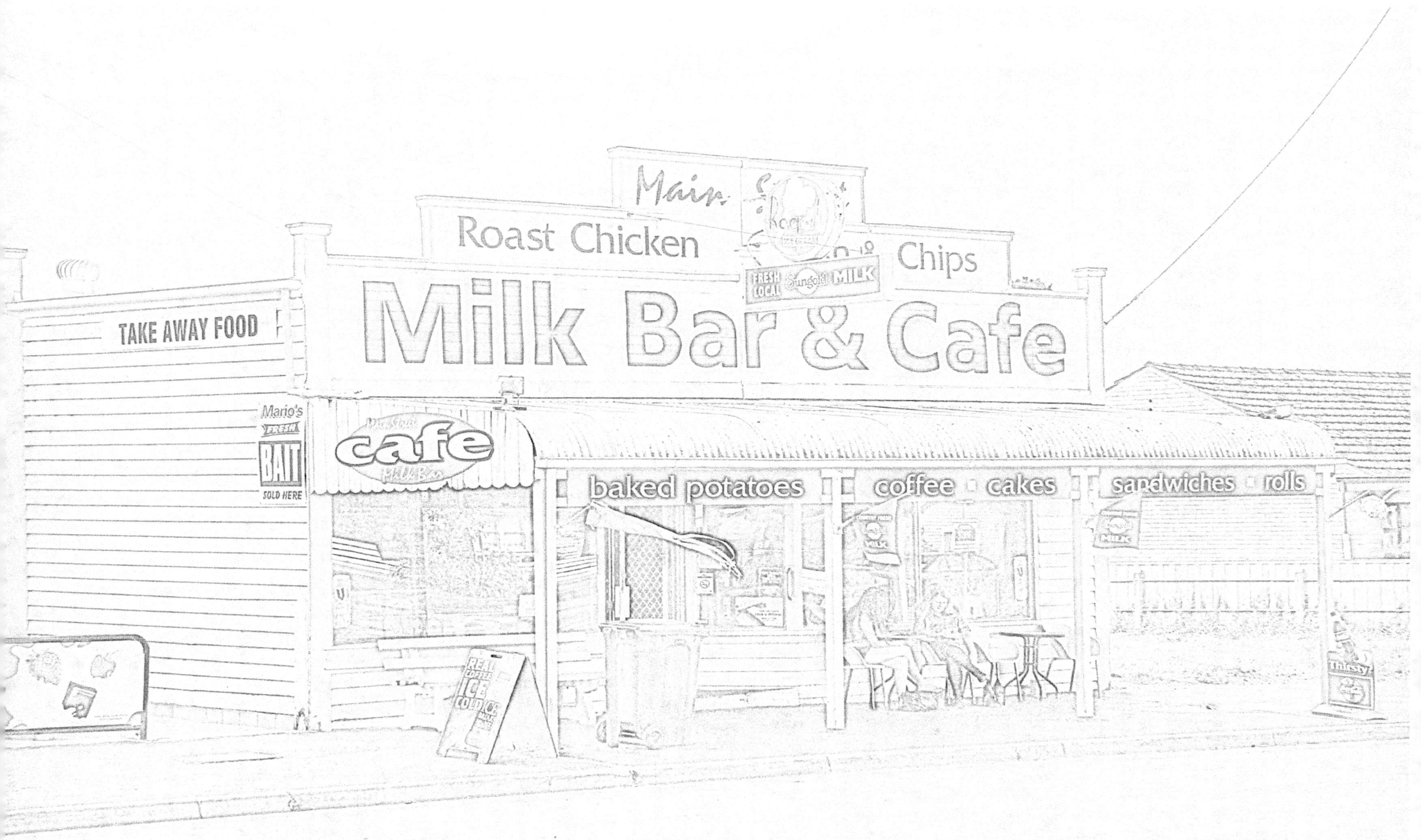
Main
Roast Chicken
Chips
FRESH LOCAL Sungold MILK
Milk Bar & Cafe
TAKE AWAY FOOD
Mario's FRESH BAIT SOLD HERE
cafe
baked potatoes
coffee cakes
sandwiches rolls
Thirsty?

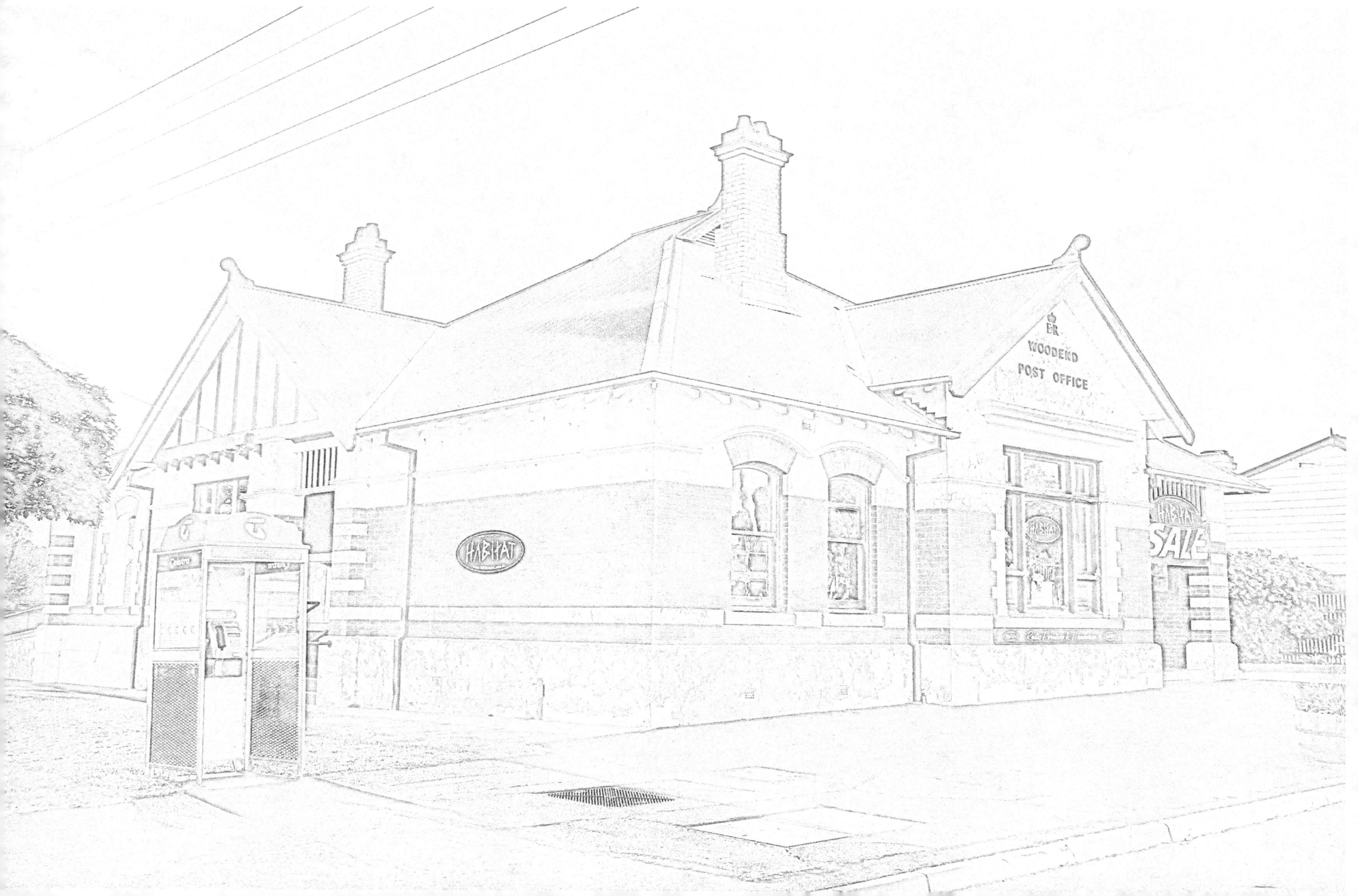
ER
WOODEND
POST OFFICE
HABITAT
SALE

www.ingramcontent.com/pod-product-compliance
Lightning Source LLC
Chambersburg PA
CBHW081056180526
45170CB00005B/1780
* 9 7 8 0 3 5 9 8 6 3 2 7 3 *